# Africa Presents The Congo RDC

And

A CongoleseWoman Chief (Mfumu-Nkento)

First Edition

By

**BEPONA COLLECTION**

# AFRICA PRESENTS THE CONGO RDC

AND

A Congolese Woman Chief (Mfumu-Nkento)

First Edition

By

Bepona Collection

Copyright © 2011 by *Bepona Collection*

ISBN: 978-0-9859230-3-7

Printed in the United States of America

BeponaBooks

# AFRICA

Madeira Is.
(Portugal)

Canary Is.
(Spain)

Mediterranean Sea

⊗Rabat
Algiers⊗ Tunis
**MOROCCO** **TUNISIA**
Tripoli⊗

Alexandria
Cairo⊗

**WESTERN
SAHARA
(MOROCCO)**

**ALGERIA**

**LIBYA**

**EGYPT**

Red Sea

Nile R.

**CAPE
VERDE**

**MAURITANIA**

**MALI**

**NIGER**

**CHAD**

Khartoum

**ERITREA**

Dakar⊗
**THE GAMBIA**
**SENEGAL**
Senegal R.
**GUINEA-BISSAU**
Bamako
**GUINEA**
Freetown⊗
**SIERRA LEONE**
Monrovia⊗
**LIBERIA**
Abidjan

Niger R.

**CÔTE
D'IVOIRE**
**GHANA**
Accra⊗

**BENIN**
**TOGO**

**NIGERIA**
Lagos
Benue R.

Lake
Chad
N'Djamena⊗

**SUDAN**

Addis
Ababa

**DJIBOUTI**

**ETHIOPIA**

**SOMALIA**

**CENTRAL
AFRICAN
REPUBLIC**

Uele R.

Congo R.

**UGANDA**
Kampala⊗

Mogadishu

**EQUATORIAL GUINEA**
**SÃO TOMÉ &
PRÍNCIPE**

**CAMEROON**

**GABON**

**REP. CONGO**

Brazzaville⊗
**(ANGOLA)**
Kinshasa

**DEM. REP.
CONGO**
**RWANDA**
**BURUNDI**

Nairobi⊗
**KENYA**

0° Equa

Lake
Victoria

**ATLANTIC
OCEAN**

Luanda⊗

Lake
Tanganyika

**TANZANIA**

Zanzibar (Gr. Br.)
Dar es Salaam⊗

SE

**COMOROS**

**ANGOLA**

**ZAMBIA**
Lusaka⊗
Zambezi R.

Lake
Malawi
**MALAWI**

**NAMIBIA**

Harare⊗
**ZIMBABWE**

**MOZAMBIQUE**

**MADAGASCAR**

Antananari

Tropic of Ca

**BOTSWANA**

Pretoria
Johannesburg
⊗Maputo

**SWAZILAND**

**SOUTH
AFRICA**

Durban

**LESOTHO**

**INDIAN
OCEAN**

Cape of
Good Hope
⊗Cape Town

# M.A.P

DEMOCRATIC REPUBLIC OF THE CONGO

# KINSHASA, THE CAPITAL CITY OF THE CONGO RDC

## PRIOR TO THE CIVIL WAR

# AFRICAN WOMAN'S LEADERSHIP

*LOVE*

*PEACE*

*JUSTICE,*

*INTEGRITY*

*WISDOM, CARING, AND COMPASSION*

# L O V E

Though I speak with the tongues of men and of angels,

but have not love, I have become sounding brass or a

clanging cymbal. And though I have *the gift of* prophecy,

and understand all mysteries and all knowledge, and

though I have all faith, so that I could remove

mountains, but have not love, I am nothing. And though

I bestow all my goods to feed *the poor,* and though I give

my body to be burned, but have not love, it profits me

nothing (I CORITHIANS 13:1-3)

# PREFACE

While the voices of most Contemporary African and particularly Congolese women haven't been heard beyond their nearest families or friends, the Congolese oral traditional law reveals that a female individual in our ancient time was always regarded as an intelligent being that was empowered to assume big responsibilities both in the family and in her society.

In the "*Kingdom of Kongo*, or Le Royaume du Kongo" for instance, oral traditions disclosed that the Queen of Kongo had exemplified the strength and the power of a Congolese woman. She revealed the wisdom of an African woman in dealing with internal and external matters. She had a fierce determination in reaching any set goal; and was fearless in taking such approach. That was due both to her innate wisdom as well as to her higher degree of diplomacy. Further, she was viewed as an eloquent and a debater woman in terms of negotiating any types of issues, and especially the issues regarding the protection of her fellowman, as well as the preservation of her land. The Bantu/Congolese traditional law confirmed the truth of the above mentioned attributes of a woman chief in respect to her enthronement.

Prior to being empowered to sit on the throne, she initially would have to appear as an eloquent debater, a bright diplomat, and a persuasive leader. She would also have to demonstrate the ability to make decisions and implement them without fear or delay. Such female individual is termed, "Mfumu-Nkento (literally meaning Woman Chief) in the Congolese or Bantu society."

In fact, the title of Mfumu Nkento was not only assigned to the female individual governing the society, but this title was also designated to any courageous female in the Bantu or Congolese family who was empowered in replacing the senior male leader's leadership that appeared to be frail during that particular time, or it could also be a title which had just been inherited after the death of the previous chief. Such was an exceptional Congolese woman who was seen fit to lead, due to those attributes. Besides from being humble and caring, Mfumu-Nkento is also viewed as an exceptional individual who is inspired by a Higher Being, and she proves also to be brilliant in terms of overseeing, handling, or resolving family and social issues wisely.

Currently, in order for a woman to be considered as a "Mfumu Nkento (Woman Chief)," in our modern society, both requirements, ancient and modern would have to be satisfied.

Obviously, that female individual would generally have to exhibit the same criteria which our ancient "Mfumu Nkento had exhibited in the past. The only difference would however be in the fact that the title of Mfumu-Nkento will no longer have to be inherited as it had been during the Kongo Kingdom. Currently, our modern Mfumu-Nkento would have to be referred to as a "Woman President." She would have to be elected by the population in order to assume the leadership of the country. Nevertheless, she still will have to prove that she is a persuasive individual, and an eloquent debater, capable in negotiating internal as well as external matters. In addition, she will have to acquire a higher education, in this day and age, in order to meet the standard of a suitable Mfumu-Nkento (woman chief) who would have to face diverse modern issues, cope with all those challenges wisely, as well as proving her loyalty to the nation.

Further, that female individual will have to be shaped by various trainings, professional experience, and personal philosophy. Furthermore, that individual will have to be skillful at handling family matters, as she will be in dealing with serious national as well international issues. Moreover, she will have to be a proud example of women power reminiscent from ancient times. Mfumu Nkento (woman chief) is normally viewed as an individual, who has amazing natural skills in resolving problems wisely and harmoniously around her family,

as well as with her neighbors. Her emotional calm and mental toughness allow her to intuitively follow her insights in guiding her close associates, who appear confused by her forthrightness. Historically, African or Congolese women were viewed as people with the ability to ensure proper guidance in others. Based on culture, Congolese women were taught to maintain a peaceful environment at all times, because it helps develop a genuine love around the family and neighbors. Women are also instructed to be faithful to the following spirit: respect, caring, sharing, justice, integrity, and loyalty, or fidelity. Our heroine was also instructed to be developed spiritually, because that would empower her to produce a courageous disposition in governing everyone in her society, and to ensure the protection against dangerous individuals whose objective is instability and destruction.

In fact, the African culture highlights many important topics such as "selfishness." What does selfishness do to the family and to the society? Selfishness develops nothing but hatred and antagonism within the family and also between the neighbors. To counteract selfishness requires the practice of integrity. Integrity expands love among family members and extends open arms to reach out to neighbors.  A heart that is full of love would never hold any mischievous purpose

Therefore any individual, who desires to live peacefully, would never be swayed in participating or rationalizing any destructive activities, without expecting to pay any penalty in the future.  For that reason, the prevention of ill consequences is another element that is highlighted the most in this culture.

The African culture, especially in the Bantu peoples, accentuates the term "respect" which people should utilize on a daily basis.  In the Bantu or Congolese culture a respectful form of addressing any woman is, "Mama or Mother." However, it has a different connotation from the word mother in the parental sense.  Nonetheless it is close enough to inspire the same spirit of respect, which a child would demonstrate toward its mother.  A woman in the Bantu or Congolese culture would deserve the title of a "Mother," which reflects honor and respect, because of her maternal character of taking the initiative in leading, advising, caring, and building her family in particular and the society in general.  Since as a mother, she is protective of what she has built, she for that matter would not tolerate any defiance or destruction of her efforts.  This is the reason why a Mfumu-Nkento (woman chief) must be an influential woman who fights to preserve her household and the social values. She speaks succinctly, and avoids any unnecessary lengthy remarks to the people around her in order to prevent any resentment or frustration. Additionally, her words are concise; this is what makes her governance effective and different from her counterpart or male individual.

Being patient is one of the Mfumu-Nkento (woman chief)'s secret of mastering situations. She controls her temper, and never loses it without justification. She also honors the word justice fully and recommends everyone around her to do the same in order to get everyone involved in building a happy and harmonious society. The motherhood disposition guides her to expand love, rather than to create animosity.

Mfumu-nkento, knows how to effectively apply her wisdom to lessen any tensions that might disrupt the harmony around her. Her motherhood nature also urges her to share with those who are less fortunate, whether they are family members, friends, neighbors or acquaintances. This practice enhances love instead of maintaining a spirit of selfishness or indifference to the suffering of others. Her integrity disdains any camouflage/false relationship, because her ancestors understood that where there is concealment, the only truth is hostility. In such circumstances discernment and discretion must be applied. Everyone should remember that the spirit of hatred around the family or in the society can be viewed as rotting fabric, exuding a terrible odor that nobody wants to inhale as it could threaten the peacefulness of the society as a whole.

Certainly, a man's heart was meant to carry nothing but LOVE. Where there is love there is hope for survival. LOVE brings "JOY" to your surroundings and a spirit of enthusiasm and kindness to share with friends, neighbors and acquaintances.

Thus, Mfumu-Nkento (woman chief) had revealed that intuitively, she had found the most powerful and effective weapon in the world which could be used to fight against, so called, "enemies", and she termed that efficient Weapon, **"LOVE!"**

Additionally, Mfumu-Nkento (woman chief) confirmed that that weapon, termed love, does indeed work, and she insisted that it is actually "Real," because our ancestors have applied it in various circumstances and had proved its effectiveness.

Apparently, that discovery may appears too simple to most people to accept, and yet, it is a big secret that many societies still ignore currently; hopefully they will join us one day. We trust it won't be too long before they do. Nowadays, many clan leaders feel that it is imperative to all the current Congolese historians to continue whispering this knowledge in the ears of all the younger generation, so that they too may learn why it is important to remain close to Nature. In fact, the reason for this instruction would be to satisfy that yearning desire to acquire blessings from the nature.

According to our oral traditions, our ancient Mfumu-nkento had advised us that the closer you lean towards Nature, the faster you can be showered with an excess and limitless abundance. Also, it is important to recall that "Love attracts wealth, whereas selfishness, hostility, and cruelty repel abundance from an individual who might hold it temporarily, so to speak. Our ancestors confirmed the truth of this statement when they said: "The ill gotten gains have wings," because sooner or later they will ultimately fly away from the hands of a wrong individual, and will ultimately return back to its point of origin in order to ensure the balancing of the law of cause and effect which no individual could possibly eradicate it.

# TABLE OF CONTENTS

# Introduction

Prior to elaborating the topic of Mfumu Nkento (Woman Chief) in the Bantu/Congolese society, we wish to take this opportunity and give you an overview of a Congolese woman.  The Democratic Republic of Congo is located in Central Africa.  The society of the Congo RDC is composed of two tribes, the Bantu peoples and the Pygmies.  Generally, the Bantu like to honor their traditions, because they believe that their traditions remain as the sacred instruments which would help them to shape the younger generation in retrieving their ancestors' values, and maintaining their dignity in order to building an honorable society, where the future generation would continue to grow with self-respect.

*How the Bantu society viewed a woman during the ancient time, and how she is viewed in our modern-day.*  We will briefly describe her personality, religious beliefs and how she actually handles her household, her spouse, and her neighbors in their daily association.  We will also explore how she takes charge of major social issues.  *There are questions and answers which were anticipated in regard to this topic.*

*Congolese Woman chief (Mfumu Nkento)*

Further, we will talk about her strengths and weaknesses.  In addition, we will mention her personal activities, and the manner in which she proceeds in coping with her daily challenges, which eventually bring her victory.

Ultimately, we will discover the role of Mfumu Nkento (woman chief) during the ancient time.  How did she conceive situations then, and what type of approach she took then, in order to resolve problems which brought her victory in the former time?  Basically, the younger generation acquires the correct information concerning the ancient traditions from their Congolese live *Historians* (generally these individuals are from the ancient royal families, and they are referred to us as "Chef-Coutumiers."   In fact, the information obtained from these individuals is authentic.  They have reported that in the Bantu society, the leadership was never limited to a male gender alone.  Our ancestors did always acknowledge that the wisdom to ensure a perfect leadership came from their "Nzambi-Mpungu (The Higher Being from above).  Therefore, a chosen man or a woman could very well lead the society, provided that he or she was from the royal background.  The live historians continue to instruct the youth regarding the proper manner of electing a contemporary Mfumu-Nkento (a woman head of a society.)

*Congolese Woman chief (Mfumu Nkento)*

Even though the Kingdom of Kongo has been dissolved, and had been evolved to Democratic Republic of Congo, this should not be a reason why a modern Bantu woman wouldn't be given an opportunity to ensure the leadership of her nation.  In fact, the only thing that she would need would actually be to meet all the requirements involved.  Nowadays, the ancient and modern requirements would have to be satisfied thoroughly for the sake of protecting the Bantu virtues.

Apparently, whatever was done during the ancient time, a modern Congolese woman can apply it as well, if she is willing to learn the role of the ancient female chief.  How she was able to incorporate her household activities with many other external challenges.  She had to honor the roles of being a wife, a mother and a Woman Chief.

*The frequent asked question*: Based on the Bantu/Congolese traditions, what would be the main requirements for a woman to be qualified as a Mfumu-Nkento (woman chief) who can lead the nation?

**Answer:**   We have touched it slightly above however, we will try to elaborate it further in this book.

*Congolese Woman chief (Mfumu Nkento)*

# Chapter1:

## Mfumu-Nkento (Congolese Woman Chief)

Since childhood, an African Woman is raised in taking care of the family's responsibilities. Traditionally, her motherhood begins from childhood through to her adulthood. From then on it grows proportionately with her age. Based on the Congolese culture, the most important virtues in life are explained gradually, so as the child matures, she'll fully understand the concepts as respect, caring, loving, sharing, protection, justice, integrity and religion.

In fact, this explains why her caring outlook is felt so genuinely and spontaneously in any circumstance, such as in emergency situation, or in any other social gatherings. An African Woman in the Bantu society is alert and prepared to initiate all the necessary support needed at any circumstance. Her sharing spirit has been embedded in her heart from birth. This is why she so vehemently disapproves of any selfish behavior around her. Her ancestral beliefs stop her from participating in any negative association which may degrade her family values.

*Congolese Woman chief (Mfumu Nkento)*

In fact, her ancestors had sounded a warning especially for that. A Congolese woman also declines any insinuation of taking advantage of another part of life. As a Mother, she has been made aware that by doing so, it would prevent her from achieving a common goal with those around her.

Therefore she chooses not to maintain such practice, because that too would go against her ancestors' beliefs. She tries to win the trust of those she loves and humbly serves by applying her traditional principles. Her strong protective nature, commands her to establish genuine peace with her family members and her neighbors. Her belief in justice leads her to find ways and means of preventing unfairness and creating mutual respect, loving cooperation and understanding of all the social issues.

Moreover, a Congolese mother laid emphasis on the importance of engaging her children in the labor field. She understands that her daughters and sons will be the future mothers, fathers, aunts and uncles in the society. As an African mother, she strongly believes that the next generation should learn how to become self-sufficient rather than becoming burdens to the society, and rationalizing destructive behaviors.

*Congolese Woman chief (Mfumu Nkento)*

A Congolese mother understands the consequences of not becoming self-sufficient in life.  She recognizes that a lazy individual is likely to bring trouble into the family which is never acceptable, because it undervalues the image of her family and that of the society.

When raising a child or children, they ought to learn that taking something from another individual "Cruelly," is nothing but robbery and would bring a "**Curse**" to the doer, as well as to their entire family sooner or later. *Therefore, beware of the "Ill-gotten gains*!" They are just like a mirage. It is wise to avoid any perpetual sufferings in life.

In fact, integrity should take the place of dishonesty, as far the traditions are concerned.  We understand that no one is exempt from this law of nature.  Any attempt to scorn the ancestors' wisdom, or believing that it is nothing but superstitious beliefs, would never alter the truth that lies underneath it.  These are the words which a Congolese mother actually utters repeatedly to her children, in order to exercise her maternal authority over her family and prevent future problems.

Apparently, the mother feels that shaping her children by planting a positive seed in their minds would ultimately create constructive adults

*Congolese Woman chief (Mfumu Nkento)*

who thereafter will maintain family's values thereby honoring their families, along with the society.

That type of education results to enabling the youth to remain anchored in their customs, especially to discourage bad behaviors, and eventually pass on these values to their next generation, flawlessly. Since a Congolese mother feels she is the backbone of her family, she also puts an emphasis on the word "Respect." Respect must be shown to everyone, whether they are parents, siblings, friends, neighbors and especially, to senior individuals.  In fact, respect is a keyword in African culture.  In fact, they believe that the children will always remember what "Mama" had uttered about respecting people; and they will continue to carry themselves accordingly.

Mfumu-Nkento's role was really to illumine her people in terms of their behavior towards each other, whether their family members, friends, or acquaintances, and especially, the people's behaviors towards the law of Nature, which was referred to as Nzambe (uhn-Zambah) also known as Nzambi-Mpungu or Mungu, all depending on different languages spoken in different part of the country.

*Congolese Woman chief (Mfumu Nkento*

However, it simply means God, the Great Being who resides way in heaven.  In addition, as a chief, she underlined respect to their family and social values.  She was regarded as a role model. In fact, she was also more concerned about the security of the land, so she encouraged her people to remain focused on the law of their ancestors, because it encompassed the wisdom required to ensure protection of their villages and territory against their enemies or the impostors.

Because a mother is a courageous individual who has been gifted by Nature to rear a child from infancy to adulthood thereby, ensuring her discipline, as well as her motherhood's authority to that child; and therefore, a woman chief should never appear bashful in terms of dealing with people of diverse levels.  Her supremacy should be felt when dealing with any type of people, whether those from her own society or any others.  According to their culture, as a female and a mother, a Mfumu-Nkento (woman chief) – (pronounced – uhm-fumu – uhn-kento ) was known to be humble, compassionate, courteous, but firm in resolving serious social issues.  She was capable in calling meetings in order to carry out serious discussions needed to put an end to any chaos that was threatening the land during that time.

*Congolese Woman chief (Mfumu Nkento*

The woman chief believed that convening with her collaborators, was necessary in resolving problems, however, she did not maintain an autocratic attitude. This was the reason why people lived peacefully together. As was previously indicated, she practiced all the good qualities needed in her governance; due to that reason, the population could not deride her authority. The woman chief had the authority to reinforce obedience to the law of her ancestors.

In effect, in ancient time, there was no such thing as impunity, due to that type of authority, the population was more disciplined and showed full respect to their Mfumu-Nkento (woman chief). As a matter of fact, she was held in the highest regard. In addition, there was no issue of gender that could disparage the female chief's leadership. In fact, her entire household, her village, and the whole society had to acknowledge the authority she wielded without looking at her gender. The most important thing was the acknowledgement of the fact that she was empowered to sit on that throne, and therefore, her orders had to be obeyed in spite of her female identity. However, it was never done in egoistical way, but harmoniously. Nobody could have derided her authority, because the population lived close to Nature, and was conscious of love, respect, integrity, justice, and obedience.

*Congolese Woman chief (Mfumu Nkento)*

The people acknowledged the fact that Mfumu-Nkento (woman chief) was assuming a position of power.  She was there to ensure guidance and protection to her people.  And therefore, no one could have possibly disparaged the authority of Mfumu Nkento as long as she was applying the ancestors' governmental system.

In reality, our modern society brings diverse issues that need to be addressed in order to be able to retrieve ancient family values, which could empower current Congolese women who desire to accede to a position of power.

Certainly, the criteria to become a modern Mfumu Nkento may vary slightly, but it would require a certain degree of similarity in order to keep the flow and maintain the same sense of dignity as it has been in the past.  In essence, this would require the restoration of the legal system; actually law and decency should be highlighted and reinforced recurrently.  The infiltration of impostors in the land should never be permitted, nor should they be allowed to hold any position of power in that land, as such thing would cause anarchy in any nation. When a male leader overlooks such a serious matter, a woman head of a society would prevent that issue occurring in the land of her ancestors.

*Congolese Woman chief (Mfumu Nkento)*

The male leader's behavior is due to the lack of patriotic spirit. Obviously, their disloyal act shows ignorance of Bantu peoples' values, as well as their inability to ensure the spirit of solidarity.

In essence, the word impunity was unknown in the former Congolese society, and therefore, it should be eradicated in the contemporary society once for all. As it stands now, the Congolese women judge that such restoration could be accomplished only by a Contemporary Mfumu-Nkento (woman chief), because of her motherhood disposition. She is ready to manage, arrange, restore, lead, and raise the broken society to its zenith. How many male leaders have the same conscience in the Congolese society, currently?

Are treasons ready to surrender and let go of their selfishness, injustice, impunity, disobedience to ancestors' virtues?

*The above has been a big question which a potential modern female leader or Mfumu-nkento has been asking. Can anybody give her a correct answer? What seem to be their big problem in this matter" Is it due to egocentric, self-centered character or merely to fear?*

*Congolese Woman chief (Mfumu Nkento)*

# Chapter 2:

## RELATIONSHIP BETWEEN HUSBAND AND WIFE

As a wife, a Congolese woman recalls exactly all of the necessary scrutinizing steps which the bride's and the groom's families had to undertake in order to finalize their marriage ceremony.

Obviously, the union between husband and wife in the Bantu culture is regarded as a very serious relationship, which can never be easily broken.  Truly, the Bantu woman in the Congo RDC has been instructed since her youth that she ought to respect and protect her husband in every way possible, and that without fail.  Also, she should not forget to maintain a submissive nature to him.  This is one of her priorities in her married life.  In fact, a Bantu woman adheres to this principle regardless of her intellectual achievements.  She takes her responsibilities as a wife and as a mother very seriously, so to speak.

In fact, on a daily basis, she ensures that her husband's meals are always ready, because she likes to see her husband healthy and strong.

*Congolese Woman chief (Mfumu Nkento)*

So, she oversees all the needs involved to satisfy her spouse, such as washing his clothing and ironing them on time, so that her husband would present a neat appearance.

In the Bantu society or in the Congolese culture, a woman loves to have a refined husband.  She is known to have a fancy taste in terms of selecting a partner.  And therefore, she prefers to view her spouse well dressed and well groomed everyday as she watched him going out and returning home.  The wife is usually detailed oriented in regard to her spouse's appearance.  Actually, she acts in this manner, because she is aware that the outsiders would hold her accountable for her spouse's appearance.  This is one of the reasons why she also ensures that everything about her husband appears neat and in place as it should look to a refined man.  This interest even extends to his fingernails and toenails as they must also be kept immaculately clean.  Moreover, the wife cannot overlook her husband's skin either.  She also helps him by providing special skin oil required in order to soften or beautify his skin.

In the rural areas, the traditionally blended oil is used.  While in urban areas, people apply either traditionally blended oil, or modern cream for the purpose of beautifying their own or their partners'skins.

*Congolese Woman chief (Mfumu Nkento)*

This is why Congolese men are often admired by many foreign women and marry them easily.  The husband on the other hand, also oversees his wife's needs and her appearance as well.  He loves to spend his money to purchase beautiful things for his wife.

In fact, it is not the norm in the Congolese culture to wait for a special occasion before buying jewelry, clothing, or any other type of gift for his partner. This action is actually taken quite spontaneously. Naturally, a Congolese man is eager to offer such gifts to his wife, to prevent her from looking elsewhere in order to meet her needs.  In other words, this is a prevention measure.  A Congolese man rejoices exceedingly perceiving his wife looking good and happy.  Based on the Bantu/Congolese culture, a man does not have to look at his wife's finance, as this would be degrading his manhood image.  That position is left to women.  It is quite a propos for a wife to ask money from her husband, but not the other way around. This explains the reason why a Congolese woman is quite reluctant sometimes to marry a man from a different culture, because she would lose this flavor, so to speak. However, a smart foreign man who decides to marry a Congolese woman should first begin learning the Congolese culture in terms of husband and wife relationship.

*Congolese Woman chief (Mfumu Nkento)*

Currently, however, the majority of the Congolese men have not kept up with the Bantu values; this problem is being caused by inefficient national leadership. Questions: *Based on the wealth which the country produces, how would Mfumu-Nkento (Woman Chief) proceed in order to alter the social issues in this country? Viewing the manner in which the citizens of this land are struggling to make a living - what approach would she take in order to remedy such situation?*

Based on her courage and her wisdom, Mfumu-Nkento (Woman chief) is empowered to lead legal and economic system of the nation of Congo.  She would know exactly how to manage the wealth of the country appropriately as well as to ensure its distribution proportionately.

When a male leader is indulged in carrying out unnecessary expenses which does not benefit the constituents, Mfumu-Nkento would perceive things differently.  As a mother in the society, she is concerned about the welfare of every one of her children.  She argues that the wealth of the country was meant to be used for constructive purposes. The wealth of a nation is produced in order to create various employments, so that every citizen could benefit from it and becomes

*Congolese Woman chief (Mfumu Nkento)*

self-sufficient.  This is how it had been during the ancient time, when the word scarcity was foreign to our Congolese ancestors.

In effect, the aforementioned view refers to a couple living in the urban areas, or in small towns.  In the rural areas, however, the people's daily activities involve fieldwork where the people in general would dress accordingly.  Habitually, men and women dress up in their clean garments on a Sunday, which is a Holy Day to worship God in the Churches.  This is how they have been trained to do for a decade.  Apparently, on that day, everyone refrains from doing their customary weekly activities.  Nearly everyone obeys this spiritual discipline.  In fact, anyone that acts differently would appear peculiar to the rest of the people in that particular village.  That individual is likely to be treated as an anti-Christ or as a pagan who probably views life differently.

## A CONGOLESE WOMAN'S PRIORITIES

For the Congolese woman, obviously, her primary concern is to maintain peace around her home.  Because of this, she is not too demanding.  She would settle with whatever her husband can afford

*Congolese Woman chief (Mfumu Nkento)*

to offer her at that particular time, based on his financial status. She does everything which would prevent unnecessary tension, or pressure in the family. Her main motive is to maintain harmony between her husband and herself, so that they could raise their children effectively.

Further, the couple has a strong conviction that nurturing their children in a joyous environment would produce joyous offspring who would develop moral behaviors. Eventually, those children would share that joy with their friends, and then, ultimately would create harmonious families and a cheerful society in the future, where the youth would endeavor to become productive and eventually self-sufficient.

On the other hand, the couple believes that harshness, violence and improper manners, derived from families who did not provide a pleasant nurturing environment for their children at their younger age. Consequently, the children develop unethical behaviors in the society. Those parents are held accountable in the Congolese culture. The Bantu ancestors' wisdom, states, "When you sew peanut, do not expect to reap corn. Ultimately, the children would act however they were raised from their parents' homes, since their younger age.

*Congolese Woman chief (Mfumu Nkento)*

# Chapter 3:

## Congolese Woman's Productivity

A Congolese woman is a hard working individual.  She rejoices in contributing to her household's budget.  Currently, female scholars hold administrative positions in public offices, as well as in private sectors. Therefore they can contribute equally to their family's budget.

However, a woman, who has not been privileged to acquire a high level of education, or the one who has no minimum school education, would still not remain idle.  She would strive to find simple occupations, which could bring some income to help her manage her household budget.  Usually, she will be doing some of these popular types of occupations for earning money, such as making and selling bread, Mikate (doughnut), Kwanga (Cassava bread), Bitabe (banana), Ndunda (vegetable) or some other commodities.  Nevertheless, the couple lives happily in their own way, based on what they possess at that time.  In fact, they remain focused on the main ideal, which is to create a joyful environment in which they could be able in raising their children blissfully.

*Congolese Woman chief (Mfumu Nkento)*

In the rural areas, however, a Congolese mother would train her children to start helping out in the field.  Sometimes her children, usually boys, may be gradually trained in engaging in domestic trading. They are initiated at the early age, so that they could begin earning their own money slowly, until they're able to provide for their own needs and become self-efficient.  A mother strongly believes that youth becomes more efficient when they reach their adulthood, if she begins training them when they are still young.  They would never sit still without being motivated to want to do something constructive; out of the habit, they take initiative spontaneously.

# HANDLING CHALLENGES

Concerning the relationship between a husband and his wife, it is obvious and understandable that every human being experiences ups and downs in relationship with other individuals, sometimes.  However, the relationship between a husband and wife in the Congolese culture is generally harmonious.  The percentage of divorce is very insignificant.

*Congolese Woman chief (Mfumu Nkento)*

In fact, prior to initiating a divorce procedure, both the wife's and the husband's families would have to meet in order to make an assessment of the case. If after evaluating the situation, both families believe that the couple has no legitimate reason to get a divorce, in that case, the families would intervene to arrange the situation harmoniously. Both, respective families and the couple would once again, convene to further discuss the issues and find a peaceful solution. Both leaders of respective families would listen carefully to each others' concern, husband and wife, so to speak. After evaluation of their concerns, as was previously mentioned, to any minor dispute or misunderstanding, both families would take the stand to restore peace and harmony between the couple. Usually, that latest gathering is regarded as a counseling session.

Therefore, in order to end the session, one of the family members, or the moderator, as it were, would states the following words to the couple, "People face a lot of challenges in life. Human beings are always making mistakes or are failing to overcome their shortcomings. However, we know that God alone is perfect. Because he always forgives us, we also must learn how to forgive each other.

*Congolese Woman chief (Mfumu Nkento)*

At this point, we the family members have found no legitimate reason that could break your marriage, at this point.   Let us acknowledge that God has won this battle, and we, human beings have failed our test.  In addition, in order to give recognition to the ancestors' wisdom, a simple ceremony of pouring a few drops of a drink on the floor would be performed, again stating, "Let God be the winner and be our victory.  Also let our ancestors be our witnesses in the eyes of our Nzambe (uhn-Zambah) (meaning, God the Almighty)."

Sebsequently, the couple would then be asked to forgive each other.  Based on culture, the couple is compelled to give obedience to their families' advice and eventually, save their marriage.  Bear in mind, however that divorce is regarded as a very serious and a huge case in the Congolese society, and therefore it occurs rarely.

However, violence is a legitimate reason for both families to consent and allow a divorce within the Congolese culture without any delay.  In effect, the traditional law requires that the husband and his wife show respect to their in-laws at all times. They are not permitted to use any indecent language to either side of the family.

*Congolese Woman chief (Mfumu Nkento)*

The couple is not permitted to voice any obscene language around the in-laws, because doing so, would be regarded as an act of disrespect. Such an act of disrespect could result in a justifiable reason for granting a divorce, because it involves the word, "**Respect**."  In fact, the lack of respect is a violation of the Bantu peoples' traditional law.

# PROTECTING MARRIAGE AGAINST ENEMIES

Apparently, in every society there are individuals who attempt to disrupt couples' harmony thereby inventing irrelevant stories that could cause a loving couple to divorce unnecessarily.  They are instigators, so to speak.  In the Congolese society, those individuals are called "SONGUERS," in Lingala language.

If they are known as champions of such activities, they are called, "GRAND SONGUERS," and their activity is called "***SONGI-SONGI (songue-songue)***," in Lingala language (literally, it means the activity of the double agents or mischievous individuals who are prone to cause trouble at any given moment).

*Congolese Woman chief (Mfumu Nkento)*

In essence, songuers are watched very closely within Congolese society. They have a very bad reputation, because of their dreadful behavior of breaking apart couples' relationships.

As a result of their despicable actions, their own lives are usually in peril. No decent person wants to establish any close association with them. Anyone who may be aware of their vicious activities and still chooses to befriend them should do so with extreme cautiousness and moderation.

Songuers are never welcome anywhere. Their contemptible attitude dishonors them. When they are detected from a distance, people signal each other, "Beware! Here comes, Ms or Mr. so and so, our well known songuer." People usually warn each other when they are found themselves in the presence of those kinds of individuals. "You'd better not to say anything in front of her or him, because he or she is a songuer, and might turn the conversation upside down. People would refrain carrying any former discussions or any relevant information, until the songuer would depart from their association.

*Congolese Woman chief (Mfumu Nkento*

# Chapter 4:

## HOW DO WISE WOMEN HANDLE SONGUERS?

A clever woman's victory against those, whose motive is to destroy her loving marriage, begins by dismissing the rumors of any affair reported to her about her husband.  She never acts hastily or unwisely prior to having any proof of such rumors.  In order to be on the safe side and detect the validity of such rumors, the clever woman depends upon her own insight and prayers-if she is a spiritual person. While she is conducting her own investigation care must be taken so that it's done discreetly, until she has any physical evidence.  It's rare for one in the couple to immediately react to such an allegation, or accepting such an accusation and voicing any argument.

Occasionally, however, some women use different approaches in order to put an end to the songuers' activities.  Since those individuals sometimes act as double agents and they are termed "**EPANZA-MAKITA (aponza-maketa)**, in Lingala language (it means group or families'

*Congolese Woman chief (Mfumu Nkento)*

separaters or killers), smart women take their stand and chase them away by saying to them, "Thank you for this piece of information; however, this should not really be your concern at this time; unless, you have a hidden motive behind it." She concludes saying, "it is preferable that I carry my own investigation. Also I will pray to God, so that He can reveal the truth to me regarding this piece of information, you have just conveyed.  Furthermore, she will say, "if you care then, let us all refer to the Biblical verses, (John 10:10) in order to be on the safe side, because the Light of God, never fails to reveal the truth.  The messengers of prompt us that when the Sun begins shedding its light, the cloud dissipates in its way without showing any resistance."This statement is simple but true. We might as well follow that simple truth.

Nonetheless, if that particular "songuer" continues to come back in order to disturb, or incite the wife into taking an immediate legal action against her spouse, the wife would then react violently to the songuer. Intuitively, she would sense that the "songuer" has another agenda or a personal interest in that situation.  Therefore, in order to intimidate the "Songuer," the wife would act sternly, utilizing her ingenuity.  She would raise the following questions, "What interest do you really have in this matter? Are you getting paid to do this?"

*Congolese Woman chief (Mfumu Nkento)*

Conversely, to the female songuer, the woman would say bluntly, "It appears as though you love my husband, don't you? if so, you must stop it right now, because he is a married man and we have children to nurture. We wish to raise them together in a harmonious atmosphere, so that they would grow to be happy individual in the society.  I do not wish to cause any confusion in my family, or to my husband.  Please depart from here immediately and calmly go your way On the other hand, to a male "songeur," the married woman would ask him directly, "Are you wishing my husband to divorce me, so that he could marry your sister, by chance?

If this is not the case, then what is your motive behind your story? Why are you conducting all these incessant parades on my property?" Most of the time, however, in order to dissipate his indignity, a Songuer individual would depart from the wife's view immediately; but on his way, he would be uttering unkind words, such as, well, "I am actually attempting to help you out, but you just appear to be so ignorant."  After his or her unsuccessful attempts, the Songuer individual would act strangely to the couple, or would become very cold towards both husband and wife for having failed in his demonic plan.

*Congolese Woman chief (Mfumu Nkento)*

This is actually how the majority of Congolese women utilize their wisdom to snare the songeurs' illusions.  This plan ultimately saves their marriages, against all of the false rumors.  Nevertheless, divorce is permitted in the Congolese society, when physical evidence is made available; but false rumors without any tangible proof are always discarded in court.

## DEFEATING SONGEUR AND EPANZA-MAKITA

*HOW A PASTOR'S WIFE WON HER VICTORY AGAINST A SONGEUR?*

How a wise and spiritual female individual was able to save her marriage as well as her husband's life from a vicious female songuer who had sought diverse means of destroying the couple's marriage. There was no apparent reason, except for the gratification of her vicious desire.  She and her associates were always disturbed in noticing the harmony and the joy which that spiritual couple reflected.  As a result, they became extremely jealous about that fact, and ultimately, they began to seek the means of destroying the innocent couple by targeting the servant of God.

*Congolese Woman chief (Mfumu Nkento)*

*The following illustration will prove the strength, devotion, patience, and the wisdom of a Congolese woman in managing her household as well as in dealing with social challenges.*

Ms. Kalendi hated the gut of a young Pastor who was so anointed in his way of preaching the gospel.  His spiritual gift appeared disturbing to Ms. Kalendi and especially, to her boss who was also her secret partner.  His preaching sounded contradictory to their vicious activities. Both of them sought diverse means of destroying the young Pastor, so that they could interrupt their happiness. Unfortunately, they had failed utterly at every attempt.

After several unsuccessful attempts, she decided to join the Pastor's congregation; naturally, it was in the attempt to better approach the Pastor, and eventually to increase her chance of succeeding to harm him, so she thought.  As soon as she had joined the congregation, she gave a big offering to the church.  She wrote a check in the amount of $5,000 and donated to the church at once.  Shortly afterwards, she again donated a brand new Mercedes Benz, as a gift to her Pastor.  She became a frequent devotee, and was very eager to help out around the church at any occasion.

*Congolese Woman chief (Mfumu Nkento)*

Naturally, she had a hidden motive which nobody suspected. Apparently, her actions were just the means of establishing reliance or to gain trust. It was especially to dissipate her anxiety. Nevertheless, deep down in her heart, the lady was aware that her objective was to perform a demonic mission. On the hand, she was being pressured by her boss to immediately perform that demonic activity, because his hatred was to a very large degree. And therefore, both of them found a better strategy of destroying the Pastor. As far as they were concerned, that was the optimum and the quickest way to reach their objective; and also to end the couple's happiness once and for all.

According to Ms. Kalendi, her preferred strategy of reaching her set goal was the celebration of her birthday. Eagerly, she invited the Pastor to a luxury restaurant in order to partake in her birthday's dinner. The Pastor willingly accepted his church member's invitation. Shortly after that, he notified Ms, Kandeli that he would be accompanied by his beloved wife to that restaurant, so that she too could join us in that occasion. Nevertheless, Ms. Kandeli, objected the idea of him bringing his wife to her birthday dinner. She immediately stated, "Please Pastor, do not come with your wife to my birthday dinner, because I feel strongly that your wife does not like me; Intuitively, I feel it.

*Congolese Woman chief (Mfumu Nkento)*

Therefore, it would not be a great idea for her to attend the dinner along with us.  Ms. Kalendi begged the Pastor to disregard that idea. She insisted, repeatedly, "Please do not bring your wife by all means." However, she suggested that the Pastor be accompanied rather, by the church's secretary who was a married woman, and was expecting a baby at that time.  While three of them were in the restaurant eating, Ms. Kalendi, cunningly, requested to be excused, shortly thereafter, advising her guests, the Pastor and the secretary to continue eating.  She stated that she had to respond to an emergency at that very moment.  She said to them, "It is imperative that I meet with my boss, for a little while."  It won't be long, she affirmed. She spoke with conviction and assurance that she was going to return in a little while; and join them to continue the celebration of her birthday until the end.  She appeared courteous and professional in her mannerism.

Nevertheless, as soon as she had left the restaurant, Ms. Kandeli, drove immediately to the Pastor's house in order to incite the Pastor's wife.  As soon as she arrived there, she said to her, "You are a woman; you should be smart and alert like me! I came to inform you that your husband, as a pastor, and so called the servant of God, has been having an affair with the church's secretary."

*Congolese Woman chief (Mfumu Nkento)*

Further, she said, "The pregnancy she now has, is from your husband, the so called pastor.  Don't you ever think that it is from the secretary's husband!  The pastor will actually be the father of the secretary's child; in case you were not aware of it, now you are; because I am confirming it!  As a proof, she continued, "I just saw them eating together in that luxurious restaurant," (*she gave the name of the restaurant, where she had left them*).  In order to confirm my story she said, "I would like you to get in the car, and come with me right now to that restaurant, so that you can be an eye witness."

After hearing that exciting news, the Pastors' wife accepted to go with Ms. Kalendi in order to witness the fact.  So, they drove to the restaurant in hurry.  As soon as they had arrived there, both of them got out of the car.  Slowly, they walked and stood by the restaurant's window, where they could have a better view of the Pastor and the secretary having dinner, and conversing normally.  They were seated facing each other as they continued to have dinner.  They were in fact expecting Ms. Kalendi's return.  The Pastor and the secretary were innocent indeed.  Their relationship was based solely on the church's business or God's business. It was never related to any physical affairs whatsoever.

*Congolese Woman chief (Mfumu Nkento)*

Woman Chief   48

During all that time, they had no slightest idea regarding Mrs. Kalendi's viciousness and conspire.  Apparently, both of them had a blind faith in that new church member who had given such a good impression at first. Unfortunately, both the pastor and the secretary had not taken the time to seek any illumination regarding that lady's invitation.  It appears that they had been naïve, and consequently they were fooled by the lady's false appearance.

Additionally, both the Pastor and the secretary could have never thought that Ms. Kalendi had been hired by her boyfriend who hated that Pastor to an extreme.  Ms. Kandeli and her boss both hated to see the couple (the pastor and his wife) looking happier than ever.  That man reportedly had been into many unpleasant activities, which eventually tormented his conscience.  Nonetheless, after viewing that scene, Ms. Kalendi drove the Pastor's wife back home.  While she was driving her back, on the road, Ms. Kandeli began instructing her about how she was to proceed in order to get rid of her husband without further argument. She told her to take a serious without delay against her deceitful husband.  She insisted that she should do it as soon as he gets back from the restaurant that evening.

*Congolese Woman chief (Mfumu Nkento)*

She also said, "You should react violently and asked him for a divorce, right then and there! Do not wait a day longer. The family members will all consent, because unfaithfulness is known as a legitimate reason to grant a divorce, in our culture.

Therefore, you are covered.  Especially, make sure that you do not look back or waiver.  After you make your decision, just implement it. Your husband has been cheating on you for a decade; and why should you wait any longer?  He had made you appear as a fool for so long, and why should you wait a moment longer?" The songuer continued, "What a shameful activity!  What an embarrassment, before the congregation! He got the church's secretary pregnant.  What good is he?"

Ms. Kandeli was so fiery in urging the lady to do wrong on her behalf.  She continued, "You watch! Shortly, when the entire congregation will be made aware of his deceitfulness, you will see how fast his ministry will be dissolved, as though, it had never been?"

Ms. Kandeli used all the necessary negative expressions, pertaining to degrading the servant of God.  Her main motive eventually was to influence his wife to be fiery up and act in hurry without reasoning.

*Congolese Woman chief (Mfumu Nkento)*

Ms. Kandeli continued, "It is really pathetic, but the Pastor has just lost his credibility and respect before his congregation.  He certainly is not a genuine servant of God.  In fact, he has been having this affair for over twenty years of his ministry now.  Therefore, you should not put up with that awful image," concluded Ms. Kalendi.  She was being persuasive and eventually it was to induce her to misbehave and that without giving her a moment to comment.  "Do not hesitate one moment longer. Go ahead just divorce him!" Ms. Kalendi commended her authoritatively, because she was so determined to break them apart.  And therefore, she thought she would seize that opportunity.

Humanly speaking, the Pastor's wife was in actuality disturbed to some degree after having heard that unpleasant news, and especially after viewing that picture in the restaurant, which confirmed the fact that her husband and the secretary had been going out together.  She was about to believe Ms Kalendi's fairy-tale or her ploy.

Initially, that narrative weighed heavily upon her.  She began to refer to her traditions, and she knew a woman must be patient regardless of what is happening around her prior to acting.  Evidently, she was facing a challenge.

*Congolese Woman chief (Mfumu Nkento)*

"How can I possibly apply that patience when the physical evidence has been presented? Should I just seize our respective families in order to intervene in this matter at once? "She reported. The Pastor's wife could have scarcely believed that her husband, a person who is intensely loved by the congregation could possibly become a deceitful man of God?

Because she was so accustomed to praying prior to making any kind of decision, as soon as Ms. Kalendi had left her, and went back about her personal business, the Pastor's wife received a different inspiration, thereafter. She thought the lady had gone back to her residence, and yet secretly Kalendi returned to the restaurant in order to join her guests, and continue the celebration of her birthday. However, the pastor's wife was intuitively prompted to go in prayer and seek for further illumination and wisdom to solve such a dilemma.

Eventually, she gave obedience, and then went in prayers. She was effectively illumined, and received a spiritual guidance or direction; she reported that the direction was as follow, "*You must act as a child of God would,*" said the subtle voice inside of her.

*Congolese Woman chief (Mfumu Nkento)*

The voice continued, *"Remember, when your husband returns home tonight, make sure to welcome him with love, as you have always done. Also, remember that there is no love in violence! Love clarifies it all. Love dissolves all the confusions. Love is a Powerful, and an efficient Weapon that will fight all your battles, against all your enemies, so called. Love will defeat all the giants. In that divine love, you will win your mighty Victory. So, think love, dream love, and live love. Love will actually clear and reveal the entire hidden scheme. Love will offer you a new vision. And, if you desire to be happy in your life, you should fill your heart with nothing, but Love."* This is what ancestors have advised his successors to follow!

After completing her deep prayers and meditation, the pastor's wife said, "I was rejuvenated, and I was completely at peace. The spirit of revenge and anger had disappeared at once from my mind!" As she was sitting in her living room, waiting for her husband's return, all that she could hear during that time was nothing, but the message of love and forgiveness. The atmosphere around the room was filled with love; according to her own experience, and affirmation. She also stated that she felt uplifted, as though, the room was flooded with the Angels of love.

*Congolese Woman chief (Mfumu Nkento)*

As soon as her husband arrived home, she welcomed him as she had always done, lovingly. However, she felt obligated to question him, but kindly, *"How is it that you are returning so late home today? "* Before the Pastor could have a chance to answer her, she continued, *"By the way, are you hungry? Shall I serve you dinner*? Spontaneously, the Pastor exclaimed, *"Oh my dear! At the present time, I have no more room to put any kind of food, because, Ms. Kalendi, invited me and the church's secretary at her birthday dinner in the restaurant (Called the name of the restaurant, where she saw them). "* He continued, she had offered us a variety of dishes. We were just three of us, but she just ordered a lot of food.

The Pastor continued, *"Actually, I intended to bring you with me to that dinner; unfortunately, Ms. Kalendi, declined my intention of taking you with me at her birthday dinner. She claimed, "Your wife do not like me, and I don't feel that it would be a great idea for her to attend my birthday dinner." Ms. Kalendi had preferred that we spent that moment, just three of us alone, the secretary, herself and I.* Actually, the secretary and I had been under the impression that Kandeli had probably planned to speak with us privately about the church issues.

*Congolese Woman chief (Mfumu Nkento)*

We had in fact, assumed that she was going to inquire about how she could get deeply involved in the church's business or in terms of assisting the church financially.  That was really the picture we both had in mind.  Being the fact that I am her Pastor, I granted her the time in order to please her.  In fact, it was especially to hear what she had in mind about the expansion of our congregation since she proves to be an active and a potential devotee.  We are really grateful in the manner in which she has been supporting our Ministries since she's joined us.

Hearing this statement, the Pastor's wife could hardly believe her ears.  She immediately realized that the whole situation was nothing, but a songuer's ingenuity.  She recognized the songuer or epanza-makita's scheme of creating a false and devilish story of such magnitude.  It was a high degree plot indeed!  She felt that Ms. Kalendi's snare was just too much for her to digest.  Then, all of a sudden, she lost balance, and fell on the couch that was nearby.  And then, she began to weep fiercely to express her gratitude to Nzambi-Mpungu (God the Almighty) for having prevented her from doing wrong to her beloved husband or getting her in-laws or her own family involved in epanza-makita's conspire.  She was so grateful to God and toher ancestors' advice indeed.

*Congolese Woman chief (Mfumu Nkento)*

Meantime, the husband stood there immovable and speechless for a while.  He could not understand at first, the reason why his wife wasemotionally disturbed, when he was just relaying a true story to her? Ultimately, everything was revealed after having a detailed conversation between them afterwards.

The pastor's wife began relating the whole incident to her husband. She said: "While you were in the restaurant, Tata Pasteur (my dear Pastor), Ms. Kandeli came by here tonight, in order to inform me that you and the secretary both have been having an affair for quite some time now.  She also told me that that the pregnancy she now has is from you.

In addition, she came to escort me to the restaurant, in order for me to witness how you have been secretly going out with her behind my back.  After that view, she drove me back and instructed me to divorce, or to find any other means of getting rid of you immediately; because you have abused my trust and that of the congregation.  And therefore, you have become worthless to either one.  Truly, if I had not been obedient to God, and to the law of our ancestors, I could have acted unwisely, and eventually experienced the negative effect of my action.

*Congolese Woman chief (Mfumu Nkento)*

Also if I have not taken a moment to go in prayers in order to ask for illumination and wisdom so that I could be able to handle such a repulsive situation, Dear Tata Pasteur (my beloved Pastor), I would have acted in ungodly manner, that was the way Ms. Kandeli had actually instructed me to do, the pastor's wife spoke and concluded with tease of gratitude streaming from her face.  She stressed on the power of that still small voice that speaks softly inside of you.

The pastors' wife said: "*It might sound small and too soft to pay any attention to, but it is Tremendous, if you give the obedience required.  It would silence any seething situation and bring you Victory. It is real because I have experienced it.*" She added.

As soon as the pastor heard this whole story, he immediately, felt down on his knees.  He humbly thanked God for having given him such a spiritual wife.  He cried out, and asked God to forgive his excitement of jumping into a situation without any prior spiritual preparation.  If I had taken enough time to pray prior to accepting Ms. Kandeli's invitation, God would have prevented these entire confusions. Nevertheless, the giant was defeated! God is our Victory! He stood and hugged his wife firmly.

*Congolese Woman chief (Mfumu Nkento)*

*He shouted, Songuer you will always meet with failure in your life. I so decree it!  Remember that our "Nzambe (God) is love and the law of our ancestors entails love, but not hatred. Apparently, you have decided to negate your cultural values, but do not forget the consequences.  In fact, all of us were instructed from early years that those wicked actions create a payback time, "La Malediction!"  So, may you hear these words, wherever you are at the present time, the pastor said it fiercely!*

Furthermore, his wife told him that since Ms. Kandeli had joined the church, from the beginning, intuitively, she had felt suspicious about all her big donations and her eccentric mannerism around the church. Probably that must have been the reason why she stated that I do not like her.  She is a woman, and she had probably sensed that I felt her suspicious disposition.

Nevertheless, she thanked God for His subtle instruction.  She was glad she had given obedience to God rather than obeying Ms. Kalendi's dreadful instructions.  In reality, her motive of becoming a church member, and offering those big and impressive donations was soon revealed.  It was to gain the Pastor's trust, because he was her target.

*Congolese Woman chief (Mfumu Nkento)*

She actively sought the means of destroying the couple's marriage as well as the Pastor and his Ministries.  Her intention to join the church was not to worship earnestly with the Congregation.  In reality, the lady was a gigantic enemy of the couple.  Her boss, the secret partner had been very jealous of the couple's joy, faith, and strength and harmonious

way of living.  In reality, both the lady and her partner were nothing, but Songuer Champions also known as *EPANZA-MAKITA!*

Regardless to all her strategies, Ms. Kalendi was always meeting with one failure after another.  Although, she always appeared well dressed, wearing expensive jewelries, carrying fancy hand-bags, and driving luxury cars, but in reality, she was very unhappy person in her heart, because she had never experienced the genuine spiritual love.  The outside appearance could not fill that gap.  Ultimately, her game was exposed to the entire congregation.  She could no longer sneer the servant of God, the truth was revealed.  Because her ensnare was unsuccessful, Ms. Kalendi, was terribly embarrassed; as a result, she departed from the congregation's view once for all.

Somehow, few years later, Ms Kandeli realized that all her schemes were powerless before the King of the universe.

*Congolese Woman chief (Mfumu Nkento)*

She was exhausted meeting with all those deceptions, and being called grand songuer, or epanza-makita.  Her health had deteriorated as well as that of her boss.  Shortly thereafter, her boss deceased.  He was known as a man that was full of pride.  With regard to his traditional law, he was completely brainwashed, and negated everything pertaining to his cultural values.  Ms Kandeli said, "My boss had gotten me also involved in his pride.  He viewed our traditions as obsolete matter.  We actually acted unethically; as a result, both of us had to reap the consequences of having copied the wrong culture of those from different societies.  It was just like being caught in the web of immorality, she affirmed.

Ultimately, she sought a spiritual help, and she was converted.  Shortly thereafter, she began overtly giving testimonies around many local churches, and in some public areas.  She was revealing all her past mistakes, treachery, deceit and embarrassments, and failures.  She spoke loud before the big audience, even though some people tried to criticize her.  She was called all types of nicknames.  She was described negatively in every way, putting all kind of labels on her. On the other hand, many people questioned her, "But why didn't you testify while your boss was still alive then?"

*Congolese Woman chief (Mfumu Nkento)*

She had always responded, "The time was inappropriate, while my boss was still living. I was not given the courage to expel every dirty thing that was embedded in my heart. However, currently, I know that the time is just appropriate, and nothing can be hidden again inside of me. All impurity in me must be driven out. Because I sincerely desire to be free from all my burdens of the past. I have been given the strength and the ability to bring out any dirty things or tricks, which I had performed during my entire life against other part of life."

She continued, "Currently, the reason I am compelled to bring forth all this immorality, is because I desire them to depart from my mind, being and world. I want that entire memory to stop haunting me. Certainly, besides from his monetary ability, my boss was as empty as I was inside. He was just incapable of helping me gain my freedom from all these nightmares! It is not that he was unwilling, but rather because he was as blind as I was. Naturally, two blind individuals cannot guide each other. I am giving my testimonies, because I desire my heart to be free from any remorse. Those filthy things do nothing, but disrupt my days and nights, I confess it." While I was acting in such ungodly manners, I had no compunction whatsoever then.

*Congolese Woman chief (Mfumu Nkento)*

Kandeli also stated that, "Externally, I know many people envy my appearance, because of my financial achievements. However, internally, I am the one who envy those who are genuine in their spiritual paths, because they are harmonious and joyful. They are not entangled up in unpleasant stuff like me. I decided to expel everything that has been torturing me, because I would like to experience genuine joy and harmony. Therefore, I do not care, who believes me and who doesn't? Currently, my main goal is to be free, and be filled with divine love, just like the one that the Pastor's wife has exemplified. I actually was so amazed to witness the power of divine love. That spiritual woman, who had defeated my ultimate attempt to harm the pastor, her beloved husband, had indeed illumined me. She had actually encouraged me to seek diligently the same thing she has. I really would be a happy woman if I could have the same degree of love and patience that lady has. "Kandeli affirmed.

Further, she said: "I had also noticed that all my dreadful activities of the past were completed annihilated by her power of divine love." Ms. Kandeli added, "I now believe frankly that Love, I mean 'divine love' is indeed a great Weapon that can fight and defeat every one of your enemy.

*Congolese Woman chief (Mfumu Nkento)*

Although, our traditions speak about love, and yet, I just like my collaborators have been stubborn to practice our traditional law, consequently I and my colleagues, all of us have actually been blinded by our human self-importance.  I particularly, mocked the servant of God.  Every time he used to preach about Divine Love, I used to sneer whenever those words were uttered.  Nonetheless, I can bluntly confirm it now that in trying to perform "Songuer or epanza-makita's activities in life, it is as though the individual is accepting to undervalue himself or herself, and therfore becomes **WORTHLESS** to the rest of the people in the society.

My snobbery did not get me anywhere.  "There is nothing hidden that cannot be revealed in this world," said the Messengers of God repeatedly."  Apparently, I was not listening then.  I could not grasp that simple truth.  My vanity spoke so loud, and yet my heart was just like an empty barrel.  It had no love.  That definitely was the main reason why my secret partner and I were so envious and jealous of any happy couple, such as the Pastor and his beloved wife.  Both of them remain indeed the living example of genuine love which has been spoken by our ancient Mfumu-Nkento. *It is that inner love which maintained and sustained the families and the society linked together harmoniously.*

*Congolese Woman chief (Mfumu Nkento)*

In *some sense, this love is one of the elements that have been incorporated in our traditional law.  Now, I would advise our people to really value it.  It is not an outdated matter, it is inevitable* thing.

Obviously, Ms, Kandeli's confession had helped many women and men, and it had especially saved many couples' relationship or marriages. Her testimonies have strengthened and encouraged several couples to establish honest and clear communications between them, as well as in their entire household.  Many individuals had been twice awaken, and more alert in terms of dealing with other human beings in the society.  There are several individuals that act just like Ms. Kandeli in the entire world. The Pastor and his wife had also exemplified the power of divine love that had destroyed all their enemies' traps.  That power of "Divine Love," had defeated the so, called giants, including their schemes, snobbery or vanity.  In addition, it had urged them to bow to the Power of Divine Love and to admit its reality.

Although some people had mixed feelings about Ms. Kandeli's testimonies, and have been condemnatory, because of what she had done in the past.  They feel that it would have been better if she had done so while her secret partner was still alive.  However, her collaborators or those who worked in close association with her confirmed her statements.

*Congolese Woman chief (Mfumu Nkento)*

Those individuals who had participated in those ungodly activities, they too, had become new creatures. Her boldness of bringing forth all the embedded impurities had encouraged other individuals to open up, and give their personal testimonies as well which have freed them from bondage.

Finally, Ms. Kandeli and all her associates had revealed one common secret.  Each of them stated that, "*The enemy of any organization or any church comes from within that organization or within that church.  Usually it is an individual who is familiar with what comes in, and what goes out; and when and how those operations occur. It is therefore, useless to search such individual outside of your organization or your own religious institutions.*"

## SONGEUR'S ACTIVITIES

HOW A HARMONIOUS COUPLE WAS INFLUENCED BY A SONGEUR AFTER TWENTY YEARS OF THEIR MARRIAGE?

As we have previously mentioned, the Songeurs or epanza-makita are the fiendish human beings who have been specialized in spreading fiendish or falsehood, notably around the harmonious couples.

*Congolese Woman chief (Mfumu Nkento)*

In general act in the same manner around family members, around religious institutions or around any other business associations.  Certain individuals are so imbued with fiendish that they have become champions in their wicked activities.  The term referred to those champions is,"Epanza-makita."

Let us take for illustration the case of a loving and happy couple who lived in Kinshasa, the capital city of Congo RDC, Mr. and Mrs. Damansi. This couple had been happily married and had five well bred children.  Besides from being a very good looking woman, Mrs., Damansi was well educated and held a position of trust at her job.  Mr. Damansi on the other hand, was a successful businessman, and was also a good husband to his wife as well as a loving father to his five children.

However, being around influential people, Mr. Damansi was unfortunately persuaded by a so called friend or his business associates. Initially, he had no idea that his friend was a very big Songeur during all that time that they began doing business together.  That man was also a well to do businessman.  Additionally, he was engaged in other inacceptable social activities which Mr. Damansi had no slightest idea.

*Congolese Woman chief (Mfumu Nkento)*

And therefore, he was busy seeking a suitable mean of influencing Mr. Damansi, so that he could break his marriage and his entire household, so to speak.   This in fact was due to the fact that Mr. Damansi and his wife were happier than he.  Besides, Mr. Damansi spoke highly about his spouse's good qualities, and the achievement of her social rank.  She was so bright and an open minded individual, according to her associates' testimony.  In addition, she was known as a multitasking woman.

Mr. Damansi had formed the habit of bragging all the time about his wife, especially, the manner in which she was managing her entire household altogether.  Furthermore, he boasted about her cooking constantly and especially the manner in which she prepared her "Pondu dish" (Cassava leaves) and Mbutu Fish (Cat Fish) in palm oil" (***Please read Africa presents the Congo RDC and the Congolese Cuisine***).  This was in fact the reason why, Mr. Damansi had always looked forwards to getting back home, immediately after work; so that he could have dinner at home.  He often had said, "I enjoyed my wife's cooking better than eating out."  It has the flavor which I cannot get from someone else's cuisine.  That is exactly how my mother had trained her prior to our wedding.

*Congolese Woman chief (Mfumu Nkento)*

In effect, Mr. Damansi was very appreciative and he had always praised the manner in which his wife took good care of his fingernails and toenails. He repeatedly said to his friend, "My wife is so meticulous. She wants her husband to project a positive image, so that she would feel proud of him. In addition, Mr. Damansi boasted the way his wife used to iron his shirts. Apparently, due to the fact that he rejoiced spending more time with his beloved family, his friend had a hard time attempting to initially influence him in his immorality. In fact, Damansi was always impatient to get back home, so he could partake dinner with his family, as usual he anticipated exquisite meals.

Whereas, his business associates did not have similar family experience, as a result, he found reasons to create outside relationship. He was always irritated to hear Mr. Damansi praising his beloved wife and children. Consequently, he began playing the role of Songeur underneath. After meeting with resistance initially, his colleague found the weakest strategy to persuade him, and to get him involved in ungodly behavior. He began inviting him on a regular basis at his mistress' residence, right after their business activities. These awful activities went on for quite sometimes. They became uncontrollable to a man who used to have such a high reputation.

*Congolese Woman chief (Mfumu Nkento)*

In order to convince Damansi, his friend had to use the following statement: *"Why do you always like to rush back home right after work? There is no need to act that way. Let us go have some air at my friend place for awhile. You need to relax sometimes!"* Spitefully, however, Mr. Damansi's colleague had found a good strategy. He and his mistress had arranged to invite another female friend over that evening. That evening was intentionally arranged, the goal was to instill discord in Damansi's household, so that would stop bragging about his wife. It became a habit after the first time. The mistress began inviting her best girl-friend at her place, whenever Mr. Damansi was coming over after work. Nevertheless, Mr. Damansi was not strong enough, and he got caught in that filthy association. Gradually he was spending more hours in that impure association than at home.

He began to rationalize his behaviors. Progressively, his family begins to notice that peculiarity. Regardless to that perception, he continued to return home very late. Sometimes he arrived around 2:00 a.m. Being that women are alert and intelligent, his wife began to inquire about such late return. Apparently, he began to find some justifications, and then he continued to use business meetings as an excuse.

*Congolese Woman chief (Mfumu Nkento)*

As a wise, an educated Congolese woman, and also as a mother, she realized that the frequency of such meetings was becoming odd to comprehend.  Eventually, the discord and suspicious thoughts began taking place around the house.  The joy of their household started to diminish gradually.   Mr. Damansi's wife and his children became deeply affected with that strange feeling and view.  Fortunately, the mother and the children were spiritual. They decided to join a fellowship prayer meeting on a regular basis, and they began to pray seriously about that situation. They had asked for the light of God to reveal that seeming mystery to all of them, so that He could be glorified, the wife reported.

As a Congolese woman and a mother, the wife was patient.  She did not brutalize the situation, because she has no physical evidence that could confirm that her husband was actually having an affair with another woman.  Therefore, she could not have any reason to seize either her own family or her in-laws in order to complain about the husband's recent behaviors.

Meanwhile, the wife and his children kept on praying without saying anything to the husband or attempting to reprimand him for his peculiarity, although it was painful to endure such situations.

*Congolese Woman chief (Mfumu Nkento)*

Mr. Damansi, on the other hand, was rejoicing to have a different experiment of his life.  That new association became his priority.  His family saw him rarely; and why was it so? Because he claimed he was so busy and the business meetings were pressuring him.  And therefore, he had no choice but to attend them all, even though, the duration of those meetings were so long. Because he used to return so late, he was no longer having dinner home.  He formed the habit of having dinner out with his new associates.

## MR. DAMANSI'S EXPERIENCE

However, few months later, Mr. Damansi received such a powerful and unusual experience of his life, which eventually had changed his entire life.  It was one evening, after leaving his concubine's home, when he was returning back home, around the usual time, close to 2:00 a.m.   As soon as he was nearing his home, approximately about 20 minutes away from his property, a group of unknown gentlemen began running after him, whispering, "Today, you must be apprehended; and your life will have to be ended, today or never! – Come on guys, let us catch him. Let us hurry up."

*Congolese Woman chief (Mfumu Nkento)*

Apparently, the group of those guys continued to run after him, whispering.  I fact they sounded breathless, stated, Mr. Damansi.  He was so terrified, and amazed to be subject to such a fiendish activity for the very first time.  He ran his head off.

As soon as he was about to reach his property, he looked behind, and noticed that the mobsters were still running after him.  Although, he had the key to his gate in his hand, he did not attempt to open the gate. It would have been too late.  He was going to get caught and eventually get killed.

Luckily, as it were, Mr. Damansi was given an extraordinary ability and strength to jump over the fence, and dropped himself inside the gate.  Unfortunately, he fell hard on a cemented floor, and eventually, he got hurt from some pieces of metal and stones that were still laying there.  Consequently, he received serious bruises all over his body.  He had lacerations over both knees.  However he managed to open the door, and got into the house. He was crawling and crying silently in order to prevent his wife and his children from waking up.  He crept slowly toward the area where he could find the necessary means of stopping the bleeding from the cuts.

*Congolese Woman chief (Mfumu Nkento)*

He was in terrible pain, as a result, he was found lying on the floor in the morning. He was finally brought to the nearest hospital where he was treated properly. Basically, Mr. Damansi suffered extremely from that accident. And he recovered six months later, but was left with several scars.

However, after being healed, he joined a group of prayer where his family was congregating. He learned to pray. Gradually he decided to make his confession, stating,"People, I now acknowledge that there is a power that controls this whole world, which is stronger than my own puny human vanity."

He continued, "I do not know how I can possibly begin telling you my narrative, but prior to voicing anything, I must humbly go down on my knees and ask my beautiful and scholar wife, my beloved children and all of you children of God who are gathered here tonight, to forgive me; if you would. I humbly ask forgiveness for having been such an unfaithful husband to my beautiful and intelligent wife, and I also have been such untrustworthy farther to my beloved children."

Mr. Damansi continued, "Again I wish to say, 'May God be glorified in Heaven for his mercy.

*Congolese Woman chief (Mfumu Nkento)*

I must also bow to God and ask him to forgive me and have mercy on me.  He is so merciful, people; if you are seeing me again today alive, I would say this is just a Miracle!"

Damansi continued, "I must confess that the reason I had that accident, which had caused me all those lacerations and contusions, and had also left me with all these awful scars, was due to my unfaithfulness. And yet, I have such a beautiful, brilliant, and professional wife. Besides from that, she is a wonderful mother to my children.  She also knows how to manage her household well.  Further, we have always been living harmoniously together, all these years.  I really do not comprehend how and why I had been possibly influenced by my business associates whom I had a high regard during all the time that we have been doing business together.  Truly, I had no idea that he was envious of me and my wife.  I was never given a hint to his social behavior.  And therefore, I was indeed ignorant to the fact that he was a Songeur, an Epanza-makita, so to speak!"

Mr. Dimansi continued, "Songeurs or epanza-makita are actually found in every level, indeed, this fiendish man had humiliated me, I could have never thought that he was a Grand Songeur!

*Congolese Woman chief (Mfumu Nkento)*

While, I was running for my life, he was quiet at his home, and was still enjoying life.  And, while I was experiencing pain from the lacerations and contusions, my friend scoffed at me.  The friend, so called never paid me any visit while I was in the hospital. The so called, friend was no longer around me even when I was recuperating.  He kept distance and was never available to answer any questions; so where were the rest of our good time associates?  In fact, that filthy group was dissolved right after that situation.  "It was my beloved wife who took good care of me, days and nights.  She was so patient and loving as usual.  And where was the songeur, during all that time? I mean the so called friend who had gotten me involved in the wrong association, under the guise of **"Let us go get some Air!"**

*In order to stress his point, Damansi repeated the following: Where was everyone in that group? They were gone from me.  All of them disappeared after succeeding their scheme.  So, do you see how the SONGEURS ACTUALLY WORK? Yes, of course, I am the one to blame, because of my human frailty.  In fact, I was under the impression that my friend was an honorable man who respects our traditional law; apparently, he was one of those individuals who had been brainwashed. They can hardly recall the words "Loyalty and integrity.*

*Congolese Woman chief (Mfumu Nkento)*

*Also, they do not remember that Jealousy is an opposite of love which our traditions evoke,* Mr. Damansi said.

Furthermore, he said the following words, "To all who are now listening to my words today, whether you are one of my family members, friends, or acquaintances, matters not.  As from this day, I must say it loud that, *I have learned my lesson!*  Therefore, as long as you live in this world, people, you should walk lively.  And especially be alert and smart, because fiendish individuals are all over the world.  They are there, seeking any suitable means and ways of degrading you.  They want you to lose your God's blessings. Those individuals want to steal your love from your loved ones and undervalue you.  Nevertheless, this negative experience has strengthened me and had also illumined me from inside out.  Frankly, if it had not been for the love and the prayers of my beloved wife and that of my beloved children, my life would have been ended on that horrible ordeal, "said Mr. Damansi humbly to the audience.

From that horrible experience, Mr. Damansi decided to commit himself to God.  He also remained a faithful husband to his wife and a loving father to his children

*Congolese Woman chief (Mfumu Nkento)*

He was no longer a businessman, but became a missionary after receiving an intense Bible Training, he began preaching.  He started taking care of God's Business instead of his traditional business.  That dreadful experience changed his life completely and helped him to bring many souls to God.  Mr. Damansi changed from an unfaithful, liar and ungodly man to a reliable, honest servant of God.   Eventually, Mr. Damansi was converted, and no one could deny it.  Damansi's new life had actually attracted a lot of businessmen to God.  Basically, his wife, his children and himself brought all types of people to learn the word of God.  Further, the Damansi family had helped many people to renounce their old and unkind habits of dealing with their fellowman.  *The practice of integrity and respect was resumed. As a matter of fact, the hidden cultural values began to be heard once more in the community. They were no longer regarded as some outdated matter to the youth of this congregation, but it was viewed as a profound instrument.*  Because Mr. Damansi had a huge property, his property was turned to a sacred place of worship.  Apparently, it was a new spiritual revival. Mr. Damansi had ultimately abandoned his worldly business, as was indicated previously, and was engaged entirely in God's business.

*Congolese Woman chief (Mfumu Nkento)*

The church administration was well organized.  The schedule was set appropriately to allow even the University students to join the youth prayer meetings and activities which have changed so many youth. Women also had their own special events, and prayer meetings, so were men.  However, there were special Days reserved to welcome everyone and worship together.  Mr. Damansi was spiritually gifted after his conversion.  He became a respectable Religious man.  His religious activities were non-denominational.

In fact, this miraculous experience from this man has been the reason why a great number of the Congolese youth and many other unbelievers had finally accepted to practice their faith in God which had eventually helped them to grow spiritually, and abandoned the practice of their immorality, under the guise of a new trend.  They began to expand God's love without any discrimination.  Mr. Damansi took his spiritual duties very seriously.  He began travelling abroad with a group of his followers to join other Christians in prayer meetings.  In essence, Mr. Damansi had kept his promise to serve God for the rest of his life. He eventually did it until the day he deceased.

*Congolese Woman chief (Mfumu Nkento)*

# Chapter 5:

## The Role of Spiritual Women in Congolese Society

Many spiritual Congolese women have been very successful in saving their husbands' lives as well as their souls.  Spiritually speaking, there are more female believers than male believers in the Congo RDC.  Normally, a female is more receptive and spiritual than a man.

In the Democratic Republic of Congo, the majority of male Congolese scholars have been previously educated at Mission Schools, which were instituted and directed by the early missionaries. Those individuals acquired additional higher education abroad.  Apparently, they had a tendency of neglecting their spiritual lives while enriching their brainpower.  Those individuals were privileged to hold positions of trust in the society.  They also received more respect because of their level of education and their professionalism.  Consequently, they became egocentric and were too proud to humble themselves by spirituality.

*Congolese Woman chief (Mfumu Nkento)*

They were held in high esteem because of their education, monetary worth and regard held by ordinary working people. Consequently, those men began to rationalize their unethical behaviors. In fact, not only that they had neglected their spiritual lives, but they also had tendency to neglect their cultural values which had resulted to serious confusions in their modern family relationship.

Currently, since spiritual revivalism has been sweeping over the country and throughout the Earth, a well known and invisible weapon, called spiritual "Love" is being viewed by many married couples.

Apparently, the women's compassion, patience and genuine love for their husbands had made it possible in bringing their husbands to humbly accept the power of their Creator.

Obviously from their own mouths, men's testimonies are overflowing regularly before the anointed Servants of God.  Witnesses are viewing how the stubbornness of those so called proud scholars are being dissolved, while tears stream from their faces and express their gratitude.  Honestly, many of them are finally accepting their Lord and Savior, into their lives.

*Congolese Woman chief (Mfumu Nkento)*

*In addition, many of them also begin to realize their big mistake in believing that our traditional law which holds the root of our Bantu culture could be regarded as an obsolete matter; and yet it incorporates all the positive elements, including integrity, justice, respect love and the fear of our* **Nzambe/Nzambi-Mpungu/Mungu (pronounced as uhn-Zambah/uhn-Zambe-uhm-Pungu/Moongoo** *– These are just God's attributes in three different Congolese languages, which are Lingala/Kikongo /and Swahili.*

Evidently, many of those individuals are grateful to their beloved wives.  They do not cease to kneel down in order to express their gratitude for all their perseverance, faith, patience, and especially their high degree of love and their spirit of forgiveness for having been previously insensitive towards their spiritual development.  *The husbands had finally admitted their defiance, arrogance, pride and resistance towards their Nzambe (God) whom their ancestors feared greatly, the giver of their lives and all the earthly wealth; as well as the giver of all the opportunities to enjoy that wealth.  Currently, because of the women's genuine love, patience and spiritual strength, men appreciate their wives more than they ever did prior to this situation.*

*Congolese Woman chief (Mfumu Nkento)*

Ultimately, those men have become new creators, because of their wives' love, determination and patience.  Their minds have been renewed; the old habits have been abandoned, and dissolved such as, drinking, smoking cigarettes and other weaknesses.  Clearly, a Congolese woman is a loving, caring, patient and compliant person.  In reality, she is viewed as a builder and a protector of a family, as well as a builder and protector of a society.

*However, when the husband proves to be abusive or violent, that would be the time when the woman would finally make up her mind to depart once and for all from that man's life, because their respective families would acknowledge the legitimacy of the cause that would result to a divorce without any fraction of delay, as it was previously indicated.*

*Please bear in mind that, regardless of all those woman's qualities that were mentioned above, and especially, her submissive disposition, a Congolese woman can be very firm or unyielding if she notices any abuse and injustice around her.  She has, on the other hand, a very strong personality in that regards*

*Congolese Woman chief (Mfumu Nkento)*

# MOTHER'S ADVICE

Besides from the previous qualities which have been discussed earlier, you should bear in mind that Congolese mothers do not forget to remind their children of the following, "No matter how big you have become in life, you must not forget to *"LOOK BACK WHERE YOU CAME FROM!"* Your traditions should always be remembered. You shall not become indifferent to those around you.  Always, be willing to share what you have acquired, if you want to enjoy life fully.  Further, learn how to lift those who are falling down, due to the inadequate support, if you actually wish to gain respect in the society; and receive further blessings."

Furthermore, should you become a leader, never forget to look at every direction in order to detect any neglected soul who might be in need of getting helped; and by doing so, that individual would also be able to help and save anyone else in the society in the future."  In general, a mother has the ability to extend her vision.  She not only focuses on one corner, but she looks to every corner of her home.

*Congolese Woman chief (Mfumu Nkento)*

Her goal is really to identify any need that could be met in a short or in a long term.  She intuitively knows how to prioritize her duties.

A good mother is meticulous, because she knows how to prioritize those needs.  Her maternal character, urges her to meet the urgent needs in a timely manner in order to satisfy each one of her children.  She practices the principle of justice.  In addition, a mother gazes at the distance to ensure the safety of any location where she had placed her children.  Her goal is to be able to identify the needs of each child, and to perceive in which manner she could possibly provide the critical assistance to those areas on time.  Ultimately, a good mother in the Bantu culture is diligent. She is known as a family Mfumu-Nkento, so to speak in the Bantu/Congolese society.

# PRACTICE OF JUSTICE

A loving mother never practices injustice, but treats all her children equally, as we have previously discussed.  Mama strives to perform everything perfectly well in her humble way for her children as well as for her husband! What is her purpose of acting in that manner?

*Congolese Woman chief (Mfumu Nkento)*

Actually, her aim to act this way is merely to prove her genuine love and create a content environment in which children may grow cheerfully. In fact, everything is done spontaneously, out of her volition.   Truly creating a blissful atmosphere around her family proves her longing desire to foster a peaceful environment, where everyone would acknowledge the magnitude of the word *LOVE,* which is in fact, a coherent force that binds every family member, as well as those in the society together.  According to the oral traditions, this in fact, is the reason why a Mfumu-nkento had called it a Weapon or a remedy that could cure any family or social disease resulting from bitterness, hatred or antagonism.

Apparently, because of its extraordinary effect in the mind of every man; the Congolese ancestors had whispered in the ears of their successors that "Love is actually the most powerful *WEAPON, WHICH EVERY PERSON NEEDS IN ORDER TO RESTORE A BROKEN HOME, A BROKEN SOCIETY AND ESPECIALLY TO REBUILD A BROKEN WORLD, because love was inspired by our Nzambe (The Great Being that resides way in heaven or God).  That Being requires peace and harmony among his people.  However, he could strike on those who are defiant to his law apparently; even the so called little gods are so frightened of its anger.*

*Congolese Woman chief (Mfumu Nkento)*

*And therefore, the Bantu society must be built upon the rock of Love in order for it to survive.  Mfumu-nkento continues to reiterate the concept of love in the Bantu society, stating that if a society practices genuine Love, as a result, Justice should reign, Integrity should be re-enforced; Peace and Harmony should be established. No harm of any kind should be done to your fellowman such as violence, stealing or any types of abuses.  Because impunity is the unknown word to our society, justice must be prevailed.  It is well to recall that the consequences of mischievousness are penalties related to our traditional law.  The malice activities are substantiated by the word CURSE to the one who had produced them. This has been the reason why the Bantu ancestors insisted strongly on the word Curse; because it is regarded as a law which no one can extricate himself or herself from it.  Currently, our modern society acknowledges it as the law of cause and effect which no one can eradicate it in the history of humanity either.*

# Chapter 6:

## QUALITIES AND ATTRIBUTES

In order to become a Mfumu-Nkento (Woman Chief) in the Bantu/Congolese society, a woman has to meet the primary requirements; that is, she will have to prove that she is indeed a native

*Congolese Woman chief (Mfumu Nkento)*

Congolese of RDC from the ancient background or originating from the "Royaume du Kongo" or Kongo Kingdom". The main reason of this verification is to ensure that that female individual would be capable in transmitting a high degree of oral traditions to the new generation without any divergence.

However, in the Congolese modern society, after meeting the primary requirement which is really the knowledge of the Bantu peoples' traditional law, which encompasses the following positive elements: love, respect, integrity, loyalty, compassion, justice/fairness, and patience, and afterwards, the individual would have to meet a secondary requirement, which is based on the broad educational knowledge. Further, nowadays, that woman would have to exhibit an extensive professional experience in order to be entrusted with the nation's leadership.

According to the oral traditions, Mfumu-Nkento (uhm-Fumu uhn-kahnto) had revealed that in the former Congolese society, a gender or a marital status were never viewed as barriers to accede on the throne. However, the following elements were mandatory, such as having the wisdom required, being assertive or an eloquent debater and also being a smart negotiator.

*Congolese Woman chief (Mfumu Nkento)*

In addition to having a good sense of diplomacy and intelligence to fight for the interest of her people and the protection of her territory were sufficient criteria, as it were.

## Mfumu-Nkento (Woman Chief) – In Contemporary Society

### As a Modern Judge in the Current Women Issues

**Question:** *HOW WOULD SHE HANDLE CURRENT WOMEN ISSUES IN THE CONGO RDC?*

With respect to the Congolese women's issues, Mfumu-Nkento (Woman Chief), because of her maternal disposition, she is viewed primarily as a mother of a nation according to the traditions.  So, if she had been nation Head, being that she was naturally given an insight to perceive ahead of time, as well as a diplomacy to handle any situation wisely, in that respect, she would be capable to resolve the current Congolese children and women's issues, swiftly.

As a woman and a leader, she would be more sensitive to understand and to better handle those critical issues.  Since it is real that women are undergoing a large degree of pain and suffering, Mfumu-Nkento, as a female, would associate herself with that intense pain and

*Congolese Woman chief (Mfumu Nkento)*

suffering better than a male leader would feel.  She would not tolerate the duration of these atrocities which women have been enduring for a decade or continue to observe the political games, as it were.  Certainly, undergoing a physical experience is more painful than hearing its description, especially if the issue is related to the opposite gender.  To a male gender, the female's sufferings and painful experience would not mean much, unless such male individual has a high degree of illumination and love.   Therefore, Mfumu-Nkento (woman chief) would make it a priority in resolving Congolese women's problems.

Sexual violence and physical assault to senior citizens, to little girls as well as to every woman of different age category are appalling indeed in the 21$^{st}$ century where the scholars have been emerged in every nation of the world, and yet the opposite gender view such issue as though it were a small matter, which does not necessitate an immediate attention.  The magnitude of these atrocities breaks Congolese women's hearts.  The entire world has become insensitive to provide any type of a positive input which could possibly stop such atrocities. This indicates the reason why the Congolese women are clamoring for that matter. They are wishing strongly that contemporary governmental system incorporates female individuals to hold positions of trust, so that they,

*Congolese Woman chief (Mfumu Nkento)*

as the mothers of the society, could educate the male individuals. In that respect, they could be awakened and try to retrieve their ancestors' values, restore morality, and rebuild the country.

As it stands now, the social conditions are not promoting Bantu predecessors' qualities.  A Mfumu-Nkento (woman chief) would actually know exactly how to ensure permanent security for Congolese women and especially for their little girls, who've been exposed to incessant rapes, sexual assaults and other horrific acts of violence without having either a police protection, or a legal system to bring their violators to justice.

Evidently, injustice and impunity are due to a lack of committed national leadership.  And therefore, as a mother who is filled with the spirit of justice, a female leader would never limit her leadership to the women's issues alone, but would ensure the safety measures to both men and women, without any discrimination, being that both male and woman are all her children.  Therefore, she would rejoice seeing male and woman individuals working harmoniously together in fostering the development of their country.  This is the aim of a real Woman chief in the Bantu/Congolese society.

*Congolese Woman chief (Mfumu Nkento)*

In fact, in our modern society, a Mfumu-Nkento (woman chief) would have to utilize the broad knowledge that she has acquired from her higher education including her professional experience in order to be able to meet her obligation adequately.  The knowledge of her traditions, together with her intellectual and professional experience would strengthen her ability to be committed in putting an end to all the abuses, which continue to run rampant in every sector throughout the country. Her compassionate disposition, her vision and belief in a better DRC, would guide her to better restore, and improve the current social conditions, which do not promote unity or justice for dispossessed individuals, or establish positive and productive international and domestic policies.

Clearly, any female who meets all the necessary requirements or who has credentials, expertise and experience, and who proves to have assertiveness along with her clever insights should be authorized to lead the country without any reservation.  It would be very unfair to undermine her ability due to her gender, because her qualities would actually affirm her strength to become a great Leader.  In ancient time, the criteria were different.  *However, up to these days, in the Congolese villages; the political structure continues to follow the family hierarchy.*

*Congolese Woman chief (Mfumu Nkento)*

*The village leadership and the clan leadership must always be inherited. Formal ceremonies relative to enthronement are always performed. The usurpation of this power is viewed as a serious crime. In respect to gender, such issue does not exist, because the traditional law had not indicated it. Any man or a woman, who fits to lead others, takes that responsibility. Ultimately, all her injunctions would have to be obeyed. Her decisions would also have to be implemented as directed.*

Usually, the leadership a Female Chief is very efficient in terms of governing every sector, due to her motherhood strength of mind, as well as to her application of integrity, love, generosity, justice, loyalty, patience, compassion as well as fairness. A female leader, as a mother would never practice any sexual abuse to a male gender under any circumstance. And yet a woman is being frequently exposed to such abuse, and at every level. This is the reason the Congolese female scholars are becoming more and more aware in declaring their legal and political rights. *It is necessary to indicate that such declaration is not being done egotistically, but harmoniously. They estimate that taking that approach would bring a positive change in the mentality of the people in the country.*

*Congolese Woman chief (Mfumu Nkento)*

*In fact, women scholars would like to perceive that truly modernization is to ensure a high standard of living to every nation, but it has not come to continue stigmatizing our traditions and our family values, in our time.  In fact, it would be impossible these days to compromise with this concept.*

# FACT or REALITY

In the country such as the Congo RDC that produces the following wealth: *ASTROCYANITE, COBALT, COLTAN, COPPER, DIAMOND, EMERALD, GERMANIUM, GOLD, IODES, GYISINITE,  MALACHITE, OIL, GAS, PEGMATITE TANTALITE, TANTALUM, TIN, TUNGSTEN, and ZINC* - In addition to many other potentials, such as hydro-electric, human, etc.., in general, women are illumined, and they have sharp perceptions.  They have realized that there is nothing to hide anymore.  As mothers of the society, they are facing serious problems with the present leadership.  Obviously, the living conditions of the population of Congo RDC today, is appalling, and therefore, all the necessary means are required to alter this negative image, which does not actually reflect ancestors' norms.  Universally, it is human nature to express oneself in order to seek a suitable solution, which would remedy the present social disease or cruelty.

*Congolese Woman chief (Mfumu Nkento)*

# *Questions and Answers*

N.B.    *The types of questions and answers found in this book were received from our Bantu live historians as was previously mentioned in this book? Those individuals have the knowledge of our past history, and therefore, they decided to anticipate all these questions and answers, during our research. We have found it necessary to reproduce them in this book.*

**Question: Ancient Mfumu-Nkento – If you were here today - How would you handle all the miseries that are running rampant in the Congolese society at the present time? Should the moral principles found in the Bantu peoples' oral traditions be ignored, nowadays?**

**Answer**: Eventually, *she would reply* – let us seek the cause instead of attempting to treat any symptoms involved.  She would conclude that based on the current social and political conditions, the male leader has been frail in terms of his leadership.  She would desire an immediate change to innovate the mentality of leaders.  She would recommend the change in headship from a male individual to a female individual capable to ensure the management of the people and the land.

*Congolese Woman chief (Mfumu Nkento)*

# Question: Why elect a woman chief?

**Answer**: Because she is dedicated to improving conditions without any reservation. Further, she is a wholehearted being. Her keen sense of perceiving things and arranging them meticulously is genuine. In addition, she does not hedge, but she acts promptly, because she is devoted in constructive causes. Since action speaks loud, the present conditions in the country show the incompetence of a male's leadership. *He has actually failed the ancestors' integrity, loyalty, justice, love, devotion, and respect test which is the basic requirement needed to build a decent society. A man has broken the ancestors' law, so to speak.*

**Question**: What happen to the good seed which the Congolese ancestors have sown? Why would the new generation reap such extent of miseries? Probably, the treasons would be able to answer this question since they actually keep on rejoicing in their fiendish.

Ancient Mfumu-Nkento (woman chief) would refer the people of Congo RDC to the following statements "Bear in mind that you should maintain the high qualities that were transmitted to you from your predecessors.

*Congolese Woman chief (Mfumu Nkento)*

Further, you must remain close to Nature as the ancestors have always been.  Plus, it would be wise if you would learn to refrain from duplicating the bitterness, greed as well as the brutality from other people, if you really desire our Nzambe/Nzambi-Mpungu/Mungu (The Great Being that resides way in heaven, God the Almighty) to keep on showering your land with prosperity!"

*In effect, you should specially, remember that hatred and disobedience to your law would attract penury in your land.  In fact, it would do so in any other land; because those elements have a repulsive force which no one could control it, besides from love." And therefore, as you journey on the Earth, do not forget the word "Integrity!"  So try to always recall that any goods you desire should be acquired honestly, for the* **ill gotten gains have wings, as well as consequences**.

In reality, in the Bantu/Congolese society, mothers act as our modern Mfumu-nkento, so in regard to the picture illustrated below, mothers state that such miserable view should be eradicated **in the land of Congo RDC**.  It appears contradictory to God's will.  People are supposed to live in accordance to the wealth of their ancestors, because the word scarcity is conflicting to the word abundance.

*Congolese Woman chief (Mfumu Nkento)*

*Why should it be a crime for these people to claim the wealth of their ancestors? Compassion, love, integrity, justice, loyalty and respect must be applied for the world to be in peace, until then **the economy of the world will remain unbalanced**.*

*While Congolese Women are clamoring – The rest of the people are mocking and rejoicing to view this image.  They are told to help themselves, and yet no one give them any opportunities to do so.*

Women are responding, "How would you like to be in our shoes? And how would you like to be forced, and find yourselves in our situation? Why and why not? Weren't we told to do unto others as you would want others to do unto you? Where are your compassion, justice, love and integrity? They feel that there is definitely a need of Mfumu-Nkento in this society who could restore the word "Justice" and sustain it.  Every citizen need to enjoy the prosperity of the country, in order to keep harmony and prevent the anarchism.

*Congolese Woman chief (Mfumu Nkento)*

# Chapter 7:

## Modern Mfumu-Nkento (Woman Chief)

## IN PUBLIC SERVICE

Considering the fact that the headship of the male individuals does not include social services – let us follow the discussion below.

**Question**: *Knowing the necessity to incorporate social department in governmental structure, what would currently be the expectation of a modern Mfumu Nkento (woman chief) in the Bantu/Congolese culture?*

Apparently, people would have a very high expectation from a mother or a woman head of the society indeed:  The woman chief would have to show her commitment and devotion in performing public services in a very precarious environment in order to contribute to the development of her new society.  She will have to set a list of priorities in order to gradually meet the expectation of her people.

*Congolese Woman chief (Mfumu Nkento)*

**Question:** *How would Mfumu-Nkento (Woman chief) solve the current problems in the Congolese modern society?*

**Answer:** She would focus on the main issues such as: "Instability, insecurity, corruption, impunity, injustice, poor governance, extreme poverty, unemployment, violations of human rights. Further, she would stop rape, as well as illegal exploitation of natural resources; furthermore, she would establish public service and infrastructure. She also would change dreadful humanitarian conditions, utilizing her maternal ingenuity.

Moreover, she would restore educational system, and make it mandatory. Additionally, she would develop agriculture in order to put an end to penury. Mfumu-Nkento would also improve environment in the Cities and small towns in order to restore her country's image. Because as a female and a mother, she loves a happy and peaceful environment, the woman chief would focus on fostering freedom, democracy, human rights, transparency as well as accountability in bringing a positive image of the Congolese society.

*Congolese Woman chief (Mfumu Nkento)*

Certainly, our current Mfumu-Nkento (woman chief) in any African society would emphasize these days on the intellectual illumination of every citizen, thereby providing learning opportunities to her People which could help them to establish good and transparent business and diplomatic relationship in the 21first century.  Evidently, in this day and age, relationship with each other is required to be transparent in order to establish some degree of trust.  Because of all the treacheries and deceits which many human beings have been facing around the world, apparently those situations make the communication between individuals nowadays very difficult, due to cynicism of the past.

Thus, people tend to decline any deals leading to deceitfulness. And therefore, transparency is required in order to attempt to rebuild a high degree of mutual reliance or faith as this would make it possible to establish any types of relationship such as business as well as diplomatic.  *In effect, people should become aware that in the new era, everything is practically evolving, especially human consciousness.  And therefore, any individual who keep on practicing fraudulence would undervalue himself or herself, because people would think too little of that individual in the society.*

*Congolese Woman chief (Mfumu Nkento)*

# CURRENT LIVING CONDITIONS IN THE CONGO RDC

**Question:** *Should it be really a crime for Mothers to request a decent Maternity in a country that produces the following wealth:* ASTROCYANITE, COBALT, COLTAN, COPPER, DIAMOND, EMERALD, GERMANIUM, GOLD, IODES, GYISINITE, MALACHITE, OIL, GAS, PEGMATITE TANTALITE, TANTALUM, TIN, TUNGSTEN, ZINC *, etc., and many more?*

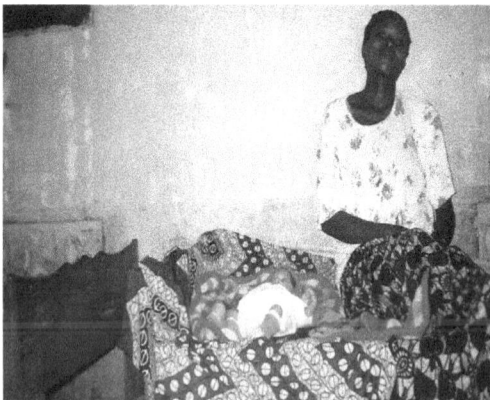

Why shouldn't babies and mothers in the Congo claim their human rights in the country of their own ancestors? It should definitely not be a crime for any woman to take such an action, in such wealthy country!

A Mother is saying, "How she would nourish this child and herself?

The System provides no social Services – No adequate Maternity.

Children continue to be born right on the ground.

*Congolese Woman chief (Mfumu Nkento)*

How can such miseries be justified and why should it be justified in the first place when the land provides various natural wealth? What is the role of a public servant in this land?

**Question:** *What would happen to a society if every time a mother would give birth, and then, she would decide to destroy that infant right then and there?*

What would happen to a family composition?

What would happen to a community?

What would happen to a society?

What would happen to the world?

**Answer:** This is the reason the Congolese women are clamoring a woman chief as a mother of a society who is family-conscious. She knows how to distinguish the necessity from luxury in terms of providing assistance to her children or to the population. A woman chief would instantly realize that providing a decent Maternity where children could be born in good environment is a necessity, and not a luxury, whereas to a current male leader this seems to be as if it were a waste of the money or merely a luxury service which does not need a prompt attention.

*Congolese Woman chief (Mfumu Nkento)*

And therefore, nobody seems to address this issue.  However, a woman head of a society has a fierce determination to address this imminent issue, develop a strategy and implement it promptly.

**WHY VIOLENCE, SEXUAL ASSAULT, BRUTALITY IN 21ST CENTURY?**

**Question**:  *Is providing security to your daughter, to your sister, to your mother and grandmother a necessity, or would that be a luxury?*

*This pictures depicts brutality and rape*

**Elderly lady victim of sexual assault**

**Below are Questions which the Congolese Women have been raising to the world**, especially to the authors of such atrocity.

*Congolese Woman chief (Mfumu Nkento)*

1. If you address a lady as a "Mother" or a grandmother would you be willing to sexually assault her? How would it feel if another man does it to them?

2. If you have a sister, how would you feel if a man rapes her?

3. If you have a ten year-old daughter, how would you feel as a father, if a man gets her pregnant? What if she's forced to bear a child at that age? Would you really be rejoicing in viewing such picture?

The Congolese women are crying loudly to the world, saying the following: "We are human beings just like you also. Can you hear our cries of hardship? Would you help us to reestablish our female dignity?" *Has it been any answer to this*? Of course no answer has been received.

**Question**: *Can daily atrocity create peace or security?*

Senior citizens were meant to be treated with a lot of respect in African culture - **Who is supposed to re-enforce morality of this nation**? Who can re-establish the traditional values of the nation?

*Congolese Woman chief (Mfumu Nkento)*

Women are just hollering for security, while reminding men to remember their ancestors' requirements of respecting women.  In fact, they should continue to honor her and address her with her suitable social title of respect, which is, a "Mother," because of her genuine love, generosity, integrity and her belief in justice and protection of her children, from any dangerous condition.  The acts of destruction are contradictory to the construction activities.

*In fact, President Barack Obama of the United States has said: "People will remember you for what you have built and not for what you have destroyed."*

The Congolese people as well as the entire world should strongly believe in this vital statement, and act accordingly.  It is very easy to destroy; however, it would be wiser to build than to destroy.  The current events make tomorrow's history.  How can the current events be forgotten in the history of any nation?  It is imperative for all the accounts of any events to be recorded chronologically and accurately so that the credits would be given historically to any individual who has been wise enough to build, and of course discredit the one who had destroyed.

*Congolese Woman chief (Mfumu Nkento)*

## *RE-INFORCING MORALITY IN THE CONGOLESE SOCIETY*

*RESPECTING SENIOR CITIZENS* the people whom we consider to be our Live Historians - is actually our norms.  Brutality, violence, rapes and all kind of miseries have been the daily experience of many women in the Democratic Republic of Congo for decades.  The Congolese custom must be restored by an illumined and a strong leader.   Mfumu-Nkento is the appropriate individual that could outlaw such as dreadful treatment to our senior citizens or to female in general.

*Brutality, violence, rapes and all kind of miseries have been the daily experience of many women in the Democratic Republic of Congo – Where did the respect of a woman, or the Congolese MAMA go? This is foreign to the Congolese traditions.  Evidently, the combination of treasons and impostors in every nation brings nothing but chaos.*

Certainly, an African mother would never, sexually assault a little boy and yet the male leaders continue to abuse women including, minors and little girls without fear or regret of any kind.  Women believe that a female president will ensure equality and security to everyone, including women as well as men

*Congolese Woman chief (Mfumu Nkento)*

It is women's hope that the current scholars will not oppose to incorporate female scholars to begin assuming the position of trust in the Congolese government, because women would re-enforce ancestral qualities in the Congolese society once more and put an end to perpetual physical atrocities, so a new breath of freedom could be brought to the people of the Congo DRC.

Because every human being was meant to be living in a peaceful environment and experience better conditions, oppression, violence and selfishness are not divine qualities, so they should not be going on in a modern era. None should tolerate it or even attempts to rationalize such act of violence, and yet the proof is being seen before our eyes. Reportedly, several individuals have been mocking Congolese women who are in distress today, all the destitute and dispossessed women, according to women's complaints, but for humanitarian reason, any individual who has a small degree of compassion could encourage the leaders not to overlook women's issues, but rather to place them among the country's priorities.

**Question**: *Why have such a longing desire for Mfumu-Nkento (woman chief to lead the nation?*

*Congolese Woman chief (Mfumu Nkento)*

We reiterate, Mfumu Nkento would insist on creating a new image of a Congolese woman. She would focus on the positive change in mental outlook of a Congolese woman. She would stir their genuine desire to be led by competent leaders. She will also strive to put an end to injustice, corruption and mismanagement of resources. In addition, she will restore the practice of all the ancestral values.

Moreover, Mfumu Nkento (Woman Chief) would advocate the right of any citizen to benefit from all the wealth that belongs to his or her country. In reality, the majority of Congolese people just hear about that, so called wealth, which their country produces, but they have never been a part of that wealth.

**Question**: *Is that how honorable leadership and righteous institutions are supposed to function? Of course not*

**Question**: CHILDREN ARE ASKING, "IS CLAIMING OUR RIGHT A CRIME?"

It is obvious that the future of a nation is in the hands of the youth of that nation. Therefore, the youth is the foundation of a nation, in that respect, the Educational system of a nation must be given priority. In the Democratic Republic of Congo, however, even though, children are

*Congolese Woman chief (Mfumu Nkento)*

willing to attend school, so that they would in the future be able to contribute constructively in the society, the educational system of the country makes it impossible for them to acquire a better education. Currently, their parents must make up their mind, between feeding the children, paying their tuitions, clothing them, and meeting other needs.

## Destitute Children

**Question**: *Why should it be a crime for these Congolese children to claim their God given rights in such a wealthy country?*

We are the citizens of this wealthy country. We are claiming our human rights. These children are really speaking out. They are entitled to receive good treatment, so they are declaring their God's given wealth. Is there anyone who can have mercy on us? God have mercy of us. We came down here to serve you. This has been the plea of the children of Congo.

*Why should it be a crime for these children to declare their rights in the country of their ancestors?*

A Congolese mother's discourse: *God, the Almighty, had provided all the Wealth to all these children. God wants these children to live a prosperous Life, so that they may grow healthy, strong, happy, beautiful, and glorify him daily, as opposed to these miseries, but who can give them this hope, except a woman chief.*

*Congolese Woman chief (Mfumu Nkento)*

Currently, the Democratic Republic of Congo is known to the World as the Poorest Country in the World. Obviously, if God wanted this country to be classified as THE POOREST COUNTRY IN THE GLOBE – A country is known to be poor if has no resources. And yet,

**Nzambe/Nzambi-Mpungu/Mungu, the Great Being who dwells way in heaven would have never provided the following Minerals to the Congolese people** *such as ASTROCYANITE, COBALT, COLTAN, COPPER, DIAMOND, EMERALD, GERMANIUM, GOLD, IODES, GYISINITE, MALACHITE, OIL, GAS, PEGMATITE, TANTALITE, TANTALUM, TIN, TUNGSTEN, ZINC* **, etc.., and many more.**

In reality, the Congolese mothers and many sincere people admit that the living conditions in this nation are unacceptable. A Mfumu-Nkento (woman chief) is needed to advocate the restoration of the living conditions of her constituents in order to return them in their pristine state when the foreign words such as scarcity, depression, inflation, impunity were non-existence.

**QUESTION**: *CAN EDUCATION BE RESTORED IN THE CONGO RDC? IS THERE ANY MALE LEADER WILLING ENOUGH TO DREAM ABOUT REVAMPING THE SCHOOL EDUCATION FOR THE DESTITUTE CHILDREN?*

*Congolese Woman chief (Mfumu Nkento)*

Would a woman head of a society tolerate the conditions shown below? How long could a mother wait to alter the appearance and functioning of her children's school institutions? In effect, modern woman does not lack the ability or the intelligence, all she needs is the opportunity to act.

## DESTRUCTION OF EDUCATION SYSTEM

**The picture below depicts the current school operation**

Apparently, in viewing the sad picture below, to the destructive and the greedy individuals it would seems perhaps amusing to them. However, to sensitive people, and especially the Congolese parents, it is rather, a heartbreaking view!   Considering the fact that the wealth of this land was dedicated to the entire population, these children are entitled to receiving a high quality education; basically these children are the foundation of this society, and therefore, they should benefit from the wealth of their land.  Why should it be regarded as a crime for their mothers or relatives to speak out or shout for help?  Apparently nobody dare to respond positively, and be compassionate enough to revamp the institutions.

*Congolese Woman chief (Mfumu Nkento)*

**The picture depicts the current school operation in the Congo, RDC**

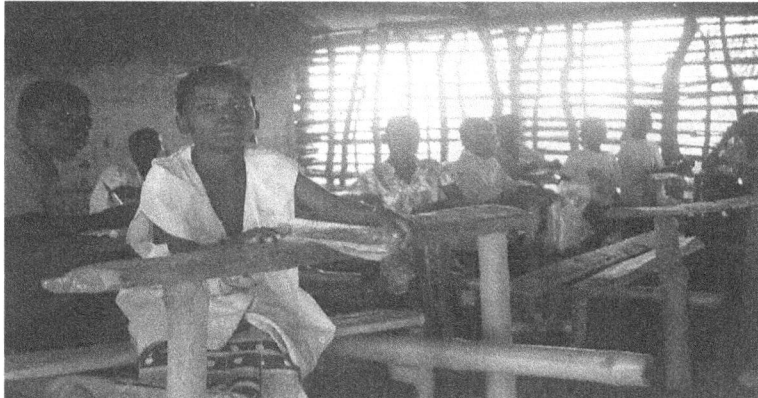

We need decent school building

We need to receive better education.

We are claiming our divine right.

In a country that produces the following a variety of minerals such as, ASTROCYANITE, COBALT, COLTAN, COPPER, DIAMOND, EMERALD, GERMANIUM, GOLD, IODES, GYISINITE, MALACHITE, OIL, GAS, PEGMATITE TANTALITE, TANTALUM, TIN, TUNGSTEN, ZINC , and many more.

**Children are just requesting a better school conditions**.

Because students are the foundation of any nation, a fair system should never overlook the educational system of the country, but provide, a decent school environment, including decent buildings. They should also provide all the necessary accommodations including school furniture required to facilitate students in acquiring a better education.

Currently, women and serious parents are infuriated in viewing the manner in which education has been neglected in the country, and yet, the majority of the children are eager to attend school, but seating on unpleasant seats for hours is very uncomfortable. Children express frustration learning in such environment.

*Congolese Woman chief (Mfumu Nkento)*

# How could such miseries be justified?

**Based on the enormous Wealth of this particular African Country, No Word Can Do Justice to the extent of such miseries in the country.**

The Congolese people believe strongly in their ancestors' wisdom, which states that, "BEWARE TAKING ANYTHING FROM ANYBODY BRUTALLY, UNLESS IT IS GIVEN TO YOU AS A GIFT.  BECAUSE, IF YOU DO, REMEMBER THAT THAT THING YOU TOOK, WILL ALWAYS BRING YOU A "CURSE", AND THAT CURSE SHALL STOP ALL YOUR BLESSINGS." The law of cause and effect is set in motion, from that time on.

This explains why the nation of Congo likes to establish a harmonious relationship with its friends and its neighbors.  Further this can be concluded that it is due to its INTERGRITY; and that is the reason why God continues to bless the country with all types of natural resources. They also continue to recall what their ancestors had whispered in their ears, "Children try to be cautious and refrain from being vicious, selfish and harsh and greedy to each other, because all these negative qualities attract nothing better, but poverty!"

*Congolese Woman chief (Mfumu Nkento)*

Many Congolese people continue to trust that one day there will be enough illumined individuals in each nation of the world that would initiate the desire for every nation to work harmoniously together. Hopefully, that time will arrive when diverse people would begin to respect each other's culture without having any desire to impose anything to anybody. Certainly, that would be an indication that people are indeed willing to establish honest trade with each other. And eventually, lift each other up. Further, be willing to kindly share the wealth which God had provided; this in fact, would be helpful in terms of creating equilibrium in the world economy, but so long as the other nations, such as the Congo RDC continues to be stepped upon and pushed way in the bottom, the world economy would remain unbalanced, the Congolese women believe so; considering the degree of the debauch that has been going on in the country.

However, if nations decide to deal with each other in transparency, ultimately, God would bless each nation abundantly seeing the harmony between His people. If the leaders of the nation of Congo RDC decide to form a democratic government, and offer legal or political rights to women, harmony would be restored among the citizens.

*Congolese Woman chief (Mfumu Nkento)*

In fact, the restoration of political and social systems would be noticed only when the living conditions are improved, that is how the nation would prove that it has actually promoted unity and equality thereby allowing minority to enjoy the prosperity of the nation.

As we have previously indicated in this book, the Congolese ancestors sounded a warning to their children against "Selfishness." Their wisdom revealed that selfishness generates anger, or hostility in the family as well as in the society.  Anyone that needs to live happily should learn how to share with those around him or her, so they too could experience that joy.

# SETTING PRIORITIES

1. Selfishness?
2.  Distribution of the Wealth of the Nation?

The wealth of a nation is dedicated to everyone in that nation in order to create a happy nation.  Even in the greatest nation on Earth, the American president's salary is known to the public.  However in most developing countries, especially the Democratic Republic of Congo

*Congolese Woman chief (Mfumu Nkento)*

the wealth of the country only belongs to the president, his close and extended family, as well his cabinet.

**Question**: *Where does the situation leave the rest of the country's people? Is this the way of applying love, justice, integrity, loyalty and respect to the population?*

Apparently, this is the main reason why the Congolese people, especially women, believe that these social ills are overwhelming to bear. Selfishness has to be eradicated in the Congolese society. And the wealth of the nation should be distributed evenly in order to ensure justice and respect to every citizen, because every human being deserves to live decently.

In the country that produces the following wealth: ASTROCYANITE, COBALT, COLTAN, COPPER, DIAMOND, EMERALD,  GERMANIUM, GOLD, IODES, GYISINITE,  MALACHITE, OIL, GAS, PEGMATITE TANTALITE, TANTALUM, TIN, TUNGSTEN,  ZINC,  and many more.

Again, women in general, and many honest and sincere people find the living conditions of the population of Congo RDC, today inexcusable.  Because of this, there is a need to restore generosity, compassion, fairness, and love in the Contemporary Bantu/Congolese society.

*Congolese Woman chief (Mfumu Nkento)*

Women are struggling days and nights to make a living.

Women are struggling days and nights in the Democratic Republic of Congo, to find means of survival. To acquire the money needed to finance their children education, as well as that of the orphans left behind by their relatives, who had been victims of that dreadful war which they are forced to pay in foreign currency.  Also they have to take care of the orphans (left behind by relatives that were killed during the dreadful war).

Women are preparing a ground to plant "Matembele Vegetable."

Matembele vegetable will be served as their food and create a small business.

A Mfumu-Nkento (woman chief) would never have time to wait any longer prior to changing this dreadful condition, because of her motherhood disposition, she is inclined to find all the necessary and appropriate means of restoring such frightful conditions, because she is smart enough to realize that frustration from the people would generate an upheaval. Considering all these facts, many people strongly believethat only a female leader could accomplish these goals and achieve the prosperity, peace and decency they so richly deserve.

*Congolese Woman chief (Mfumu Nkento)*

In fact, with respect to transparency in dealing with both genders, male and female in the Congo, women frequently refer to the following quotes below:

*American President Abraham Lincoln stated, "You can fool some of the people all of the time and all of the people some of the time, but you cannot fool all of the people all of the time."*

Many women have been fooled for a long time in our Country, but the time has come for women to speak out and assert, "Women will no longer be fooled and treated like disposable materials, which after use are destroyed and dumped in the garbage". Since Congolese men have ignored their women's pleas, Congolese women are now imploring the women of the world to hear their screaming in pain.  They had experienced enough miseries, and that is sufficient!" They've waited patiently, hoping and believing that a male Congolese leader would be compassionate enough to be able to improve their living conditions. They also would expect a male Congolese leader to practice their ancestors' traditions of addressing a woman with her title of respect and honor as" Mother of the society" as practiced years ago.

However the male Congolese leaders have turned a blind eye to their ancestral practices and traditions.  Consequently, women have

*Congolese Woman chief (Mfumu Nkento)*

become nothing within this nation, except tools of pleasure without regard to their humanity; they've been exposed to horrific sexual assaults regardless of their age from little girls through senior citizens. Why should such issue be concealed?

**Question**: *Who do you suppose is causing all of these abuses, women?*

**Answer**: *No, it is a male individual.-who refuses to remember the value of a woman, the mother of the Bantu/Congolese society in this new era.*

This long national nightmare must be ended. This is the main reason why every decent, law-abiding Congolese woman is clamoring for a woman leader to be currently. Women are saying: "We want to restore our human rights, human respect, justice, protection, integrity, loyalty and generosity in our society. We are tired of seeing everything around us is being destroyed. What future will our children have?

In developing countries such as the Democratic Republic of Congo, the leader should take this statement very seriously. They should focus all their energies in building, re-establishing and maintaining the ancestral values and traditions of our country, rather than destroying what was previously built. People would be enthusiastic

*Congolese Woman chief (Mfumu Nkento)*

about seeing constructive activities, giving hope for the future, instead of destructive activities that build nothing.

## WATER SHORTAGE

**HOW WOULD WOMAN CHIEF HANDLE THE ISSUE OF WATER SHORTAGE?**

She would remind the citizens of this country that *GOD HAS GIVEN THIS COUNTRY SEVERAL SPRINGS OR FOUNTAINS – LET US CLEAN AND DEVELOP ALL OF THEM SO THAT WE CAN HAVE CLEAN DRINKING WATER – LET US ALSO KEEP OUR RIVERS AND BROOKS CLEAN SO THAT WE CAN BE ABLE TO WASH OUR BODIES FROM THE CLEAN RUNNING BROOKS AND RIVERS.*

The Creator of this nation as well as of every nation has provided essentially all the basic needs required for individuals to live on this Earth comfortably.  It would actually be a crime to deprive those basic needs to the citizens, especially water, because they have been given to us freely.  In fact, they are the gifts of God.  They were given to the people of Congo in order to be used permanently.

Any wise leader would in effect, focus in developing every water fountain in the land and ensure protection of their rivers and brooks

*Congolese Woman chief (Mfumu Nkento)*

in order to improve the living conditions of the people, as opposed to maintaining unnecessary perpetual miseries.

Currently, miseries in the Congo RDC are overwhelmed, as it has been indicated previously! People have no clean water – either to drink or to wash themselves. And yet, the country has several water fountains which need to be developed and provide clean water to the constituents. *LET US ALSO KEEP OUR RIVERS CLEAN AND WASH OUR BODIES FROM THE CLEAN RUNNING BROOKS AND RIVERS.*

**MFUMU-NKENTO OF THE FORMER TIME KEPT ENVIRONMENTAL CLEAN -**

This image needs to be restored. The country has enough resources to alter such image.

Such situation urges the change of leadership from a male to a woman chief (Mfumu Nkento).

Women are really frustrated with such a deplorable sight. They feel that a weak male leader should definitely retire at the present time, because he is being viewed as a dreamer, and also as a blind man, who seems not to perceive what is actually happening in the world around him and his constituents.

*Congolese Woman chief (Mfumu Nkento)*

Indifference attitude towards the needs of the population would create a disturbance in the society which might affect or interrupt the governance of that leader. The divine right of free man must be honored in order to prevent people's annoyance.

In a country that produces the following wealth: ASTROCYANITE, COBALT, COLTAN, COPPER, DIAMOND, EMERALD, GERMANIUM, GOLD, IODES, GYISINITE, MALACHITE, OIL, GAS, PEGMATITE TANTALITE, TANTALUM, TIN, TUNGSTEN, ZINC, *and plu*s other potentials, such as hydro-electric human potentials as well as good climate for agriculture.  Since there is no scarcity in terms of resources, what the country needs currently in order to retrieve his ancestral dignity is a proper leadership or a competence, mature individual, who exhibits high qualities and qualifications.  Further an individual, who is a native of Congo, anchored deep in his traditional law, because he fears his Nzambe (the Great Being who dwells way in heaven).  Such leader would govern wisely, because he would know the consequence of being defiant or of breaking the law of his or her ancestors. No human being likes to be treated unfairly, as the Messengers of God had stated, "Treachery and Deceit in high places has brought the distrust of the mass of mankind and they do not known upon whom they

*Congolese Woman chief (Mfumu Nkento)*

can depend." In a country that has full of abundance, but practices selfishness and indifference to the sufferings of others, its inequalities and injustices obviously can no longer be tolerated anywhere. . It is understandable, it should not be considered as a crime for a citizen to declare a part of the whole, because it is his or her human rights.

## THE NEED OF SOCIAL SERVICES

### Living Condition of Senior Citizens in the Congo RDC

This woman in fact, has to depend on her own efforts in the attempt to make a living.  She is striving to make ends meet.  Life has been extremely awful due to the lack of social Services, in such a wealthy country.  Mfumu-Nkento (woman chief) would never accept seeing these types of situations which do not reflect any positive elements that are found in the Bantu/Congolese traditional law.

In fact, the presence of selfishness in the current Bantu peoples' society indicates defiance of their law of compassion.  Their ancestors did not know such as negative image.  There is no justification whatsoever in the land which has plenty of resources.  Scholars of the 21st Century argue fiercely that attempting to instill the word scarcity

*Congolese Woman chief (Mfumu Nkento)*

in the mentality of the people when those individuals have been aware that the land produces plenty of resources is a crime, indeed.

A brave Mfumu-Nkento, in that respect, would not let her fellowman to be entangled up in such implication. As it has been previously discussed, since the mother's role is to illumine her children and not to create any confusion to their beliefs, she would continue to apply her authority in order to stop any activities which would once again seek to brainwash the people in the attempt to conceal the reality.

So, as a woman head of a society, she would never overlook socio-economic matters and be enmeshed and distracted in general discussions with the world media thereby neglecting the immediate needs of the people who have entrusted her with that authority. As a bright diplomat, to a woman head of a nation, the sociopolitical factors would be handled wisely, bearing in mind that the unnecessary long political talks which do not result to any satisfactory and tangible actions become useless, and redundant for the people to hear. So, in the long run people lose hope and trust in the leader.

Therefore economic miseries in a wealthy land should not prevail, because there is no element that could possibly sustain it.

*Congolese Woman chief (Mfumu Nkento)*

In fact, the younger generation has found no reference whatsoever regarding such miseries, in their traditional law, as far as the Kongo kingdom is concerned.  According to the Bantu peoples' oral traditions, the State of Kongo was well developed prior to the arrival of the first European missionaries in 15th century.  Therefore, it could still go back to its pristine state, and eventually eradicate the word scarcity which has no justification, so to speak.

*The picture below depicts current living condition of senior citizens. This elderly lady, in fact there are many more struggling in raising their grandchildren in this land.*

This lady is sifting a small amount of cassava flour.  One portion will be used to feed her 8 grandsons, (All are orphans children of war victims) - Whereas another tiny portion would be sold per cup, in order to acquire some tuition money.  She is facing a dilemma – For 1 cup of flour, she charges roughly a quarter when translating in $.  She has eight grandchildren who must attend school.  The school's tuition for each child amounts to $50. 00 (fifty) per month (in foreign currency).

*Congolese Woman chief (Mfumu Nkento)*

*Question* – How many cups of flour can she sell to amount to $50.00 x 8 = $400.00 a month?

There is no public schools in this country– Therefore, children are sent back home, because their grandmother cannot afford the tuition cost.

***Consequences - Children cry, because they want to attend school.*** On the other hand, their grandmother also cries, because she can't afford it and has no support or help from any source whatsoever. And yet, there are several individuals in this society who are holding millions of dollars in their homes – while the rest of the population is starving to death. Amazingly, how they continue to mock people such as this grandmother and her 8 grandchildren, without any slightest of consideration or compassion. **Can the above image be really scoffed at in our modern society?**

*Question*: How can the population rejoice in such miseries and selfishness? Upon whom shall the people depend on? How many houses can somebody live in per day? How many cars can anyone drive per hour? How many pair of shoes can somebody wear per hour? How many pounds of beef can somebody eat an hour? How many parties or receptions can anyone give a day in order to use up all that wealth accumulated?

*Congolese Woman chief (Mfumu Nkento)*

And also, *how many trunks of paper money or coin can an individual bring with him or her when life ends in this world?* **To the above question, let everyone finds his own or her own answer.**

Evidently, people conceive things differently, based on their cultures. This is why a brave woman in the Bantu/Congolese culture would continue to advise her children, male or female that choosing to practice selfishness over generosity and compassion would never bring you a permanent happiness in life. It would rather create antagonism, resentment and insecurity around you.

Apparently, this is the reason why a mother of the Bantu peoples' society would continue to strive in restoring the morality of her people; in order to put an end to anything that appear to be unethical such as selfishness, corruption, injustice, and impunity, as well as a despotic or ruthless political system in our contemporary era.

*Congolese Woman chief (Mfumu Nkento)*

# Chapter 8:

## STREET CHILDREN

Basically, oral traditions had not transmitted any issue regarding street children; eventually such thing did not exist in ancient society. The fact that people practiced a spirit of solidarity, family members were held very close to each other's heart.  All the incoming children in the family, starting from brother, sister, nieces, nephews, and cousins all of them belonged to one big family.  And so, were mothers, aunts, uncles and grandparents were always considered as a composition of one big family.  This can be further explained with respect to family structure in the Bantu/Congolese culture.

There are two main tendencies, as it were; that is the practice of either matriarchal or patriarchal family system.  In fact, matriarchal system in the Bantu culture is referred to the fact that children belong to maternal side of the family.  In this particular system, whether a senior man or a senior woman are permitted to become head of family.

*Congolese Woman chief (Mfumu Nkento)*

It would be so, provided that that individual exemplifies all the necessary qualities required by the traditional law, as it was previously discussed. Further, we would like to highlight the fact that in order to become head of family or a clan leader, an individual does not necessarily have to be old in terms of his or her age. It simply means that the individual is the older child as far as the family hierarchy is concerned. In contrast, patriarchal system, in the Bantu/Congolese family system is referred to the fact that, the children belong to the father's side. Usually, in patriarchal family system, a man is the head of a clan or a clan chief.

Generally, there is a strong coherence between the family members. Therefore, if one of them gets in trouble or faces a serious problem, the whole family gets affected, so to speak. Consequently, each person feels obligated to bring all the necessary support required in order to resolve that problem swiftly. In fact, African families or Congolese families in particular had always emphasized the spirit of unity or collaboration. And therefore, an orphan or any child is never pushed asides, even though his or her biological parents are deceased the child never felt abandoned, unless that child has no distant relative who could assume the responsibility in rearing it.

*Congolese Woman chief (Mfumu Nkento)*

Otherwise the distant relatives would feel obligated to foster that child, lovingly, until it reaches the maturity age.  In the future, that child will also maintain the same disposition.  It will place the love of its family first among other things.

Nowadays however, our modern society has brought an unusual social dilemma whose remedy has been so far unknown to the current Congolese male leaders.  Could people speculate the reason of such ignorance? Could it be because of the fact that the current leadership has fallen in the hands of impostors and treasons, who are just focusing their entire minds and beings in amassing the country wealth for self-interest, due to lack of patriotism and also to the lack of knowledge of the people' culture? Or, it is just because the present male leaders feel possibly threatened by the evolving of the new generation, especially their brainpower?

The majority of women are concerned with street children's issues, which the male leaders or even religious institutions do not seem to touch or discuss in order to provide any assistance to those children. And yet the number of those street children has been increasing considerably due to the dreadful war in the Congo RDC.

*Congolese Woman chief (Mfumu Nkento)*

Evidently, war has brought diverse predicaments in the Congolese society.  After the loss of their parents, many teens fled from rural to urban areas in order to seek protection and opportunities.

Unfortunately, these children found no support or guidance whatsoever; as a result, they join street children.  *Based on the survey conducted in Kinshasa on April 2010, out of 10 street children, sixty seven percent (67%) stated that they are orphans, both of their parents had been the victims of that horrible war which has been devastating human lives in the Congo RDC for a decade, whereas twenty-three percent (23%) stated that they left their homes because parents were experiencing financial hardship.  Parents are actually under stress and are unable to provide for them.*

*Ten percent (10%) replied that they had to leave their homes, because they were being abused by either a step father or by a step mother. Presently, a woman in the Congo has become a breadwinner while the father continues to seek employment that does not exist anywhere.  The frightful war has brought a fundamental change in Congolese families.  Children have been experiencing discordant environments, and constant quarrels.*

*Congolese Woman chief (Mfumu Nkento)*

*Because they realize that they have no viable and loving homes to return to daily, they choose therefore, to live outside of their homes, and join street children.  They have been certainly exposed to every kind of risks, eventually.  Consequently, they exhibit violent or disruptive behavior towards authority or even innocent individuals on the road.*

***To the question: How do you survive?** In fact, 99% of these children had given similar answer such as, "We do things which we would have never done under any normal circumstances.  Since we receive no kind of assistance from either our government or from the religious leaders, in order for us to eat, we have to steal from somewhere."  **As far as clothing is concerned**, the teens replied, "Since no leader believes that are bodies are developing and we need to have them covered, we therefore, feel obligated to steal clothes from anyway we can in order to cover ourselves.*

*As you can notice, not even a single leader had ever thought to offer us any shelte; whether it rains or it shines, we have no place to run to, but stay out here. People are inclined to condemn our violent actions. They call us criminals, and they warn each other to be cautious, and beware of those violent and criminal street children.*

*Congolese Woman chief (Mfumu Nkento)*

*Do you really believe that we want to live out here, suffering, and conducting immoral activities, which is opposite to our culture? Of course not, we deserve to live decently like any other citizens. We need to acquire good education/Training, and be able to own homes and luxury cars and settle down like all those successful people.* **Aren't we the citizens of Congo RDC?**

*In effect, we are not the children of impostors, but rather the successors or the heirs of the "Royaume du Kongo"(Kongo Kingdom) – While this matter appears as though it were a small matter to all of you who keep on deriding us; it is an enormous problem to us! We are addressing to those who are practicing selfishness, we will utilize all the necessary means required in order for us to survive, as long as God continues to maintain His breath in us."*

**Question***: People say street children are very impolite and arrogant – is that true?*

**Answer***: Why should we be polite, and polite to whom? And why shouldn't we be arrogant?- The so called leaders eat three meals or more per day, whereas, street children spend days without anything in our stomach.*

*Congolese Woman chief (Mfumu Nkento)*

*So, why shouldn't street children be brazen? You address us as street children, just because we have no shelter, don't you?  Who is that individual in this country that could deserve our respect? When they are driving luxury cars and buying houses that cost from $100,000-$800,000 in this country and abroad, and ignoring the fact that we are native of Congo, and yet, we are living out here without anyone thinking about building us any shelter or offering us any food.  Is that generosity or selfishness? And yet, many individuals possess plenty of money, big sum of money, from twenty millions dollars – hundred millions in their home, as we hear them competing with each other. Where are we standing at between those individuals and their bloody wealth?*

*Street children continued, "When would those leaders show the spirit of patriotism? All they do is to travel abroad and invest in those countries, instead of creating local companies in order to give us opportunity to work so that we too could earn a living, and be self-sufficient as our culture requires. So, why shouldn't we be blatant or arrogant to them?  In fact, we address all of them by their names, because they have no consideration to common people. They are not leaders as far as we are concerned.*

*Congolese Woman chief (Mfumu Nkento)*

*Their stolen money would not buy our respect either. We know they are fearful of street children, well if it is so, they deserve experiencing our violent actions due to their injustice and selfishness, which violates our traditional law.*

*Street children continued to argue, "If being in lack and limitation is a good thing, and why then, those individuals who have accumulated the wealth of the country, dishonestly grow bitter and ill when their investments abroad fail them? How do they feel when few years later, they lose those huge houses in the foreign lands, which they had eagerly paid in full, without knowing the country's Real Estate law (Insurance involves)? Isn't that the confirmation of our ancestors' warning against the ill-gotten gains, which generate recurrence Curse?*

Our live historians are alleging that our former Nfumu-Nkento (woman chief or woman head of society), due to her motherhood disposition, if she would have been governing our society today, she would have never neglected the issue of street children or any other social issues reflecting to our modern life.

She apparently would have made it one of her priorities, and would have utilized all her ingenuity in identifying the cause of this problem, and then developing appropriate means of treating this illness thereby implementing them in order to restore the family values and meet the standard of our modern society.

*Congolese Woman chief (Mfumu Nkento)*

Among modern Congolese women, there are many who are still anchored in their traditions, so they believe strongly in preserving the family values.  Women are really concerned about the wellbeing of the current youth.  Certainly, among these children are many who had high aspirations since childhood, apparently their aspirations are being smothered, so to speak, due to the fact that no leader is offering them any opportunity to evolve.  Evidently, they are frustrated.  Arresting and beating them is by no means the worst solution.

How can those street children hold leaders in highest regard? Women are also worried about safety of everyone involved in the society, because those children are actually growing without any direction or orientation, while fair governance could provide a possible assistance in shaping adolescence and helping them remain focused on their set goals. How could anybody blame them to their violence or immorality behaviors when the leaders have actually killed their ambitions?

In essence, people are prone to condemn the behaviors of street children.  However, their arguments are valid.  True, economic hardship due to the incessant war in the country keeps on generating violence at every level.

*Congolese Woman chief (Mfumu Nkento)*

On the other hand, selfishness and lack of control of the youth generate violence in the society.  Street children argue, "We are the citizens of such wealthy country, filled with God's natural resources. We deserve to be sheltered, fed, clothes and especially, we are in a need of receiving diverse training/education in order to broaden our intellectual, moral, spiritual and cultural knowledge.

Evidently, they are definitely not going to acquire such education by living on the streets.  While the leaders and the wealthy individuals continue to scoff at them and put all kinds of labels on them, harass and sentenced them.  Women argue that such approach is derisory. Unfortunately, they are actually developing a society of aggressive individuals who eventually must utilize all the necessary and unacceptable means of survival thereby attacking the greedy individuals if need be.  Sorry to say, because they are in a desperate need, they would even attack anyone in order to have something to eat.  This is the reason why the Congolese traditions highlight ancestral virtues.  In fact, the opposite of these good qualities, ultimately generate nothing else, but hostility and chaos in the society.

*Congolese Woman chief (Mfumu Nkento)*

Naturally, violence in the society would make it hard for greedy individuals to enjoy all the wealth that they had dishonestly accumulated, by depraving their fellowman from their God's given freedom.

Clearly, street children are growing unhappily, because they are aggravated with the current management.  The observers state that, "Watch out, street children are dangerous, impertinent, arrogant, brazen and violent."  Naturally, ninety-nine percent (99%) have been expressing themselves without any reservation, while one percent (1%) just refuses to communicate with anyone; they are so infuriated with the governmental system that does not seem to realize that **SELFISHNESS** is against the Bantu/Congolese traditions.  They are frustrated with the leader that is potentially able to alter the living conditions for these people, and yet, unwilling to take any positive action.

It is difficult to conceal the truth regarding oral traditions and culture, because many among those street children some of them actually know their traditional law or principles.  They are tired of being spectators of those greedy individuals.


*Congolese Woman chief (Mfumu Nkento)*

Obviously, many people by lack of wisdom view them violent and continue to put all kinds of labels on them; but if so, they are only declaring their human rights, because they are descendents of the Kingdom of Kongo, and above all, they are the children of the most Higher Being, Nzambe, or God, and therefore, they deserve to be treated right, with justice and respect in order to prevent anarchism in the society.

### WHY ARE THE CONGOLESE WOMEN HOLLERING?

The former illustration shows the main issue, why the Congolese women are hollering and requesting a Mfumu-Nkento (Woman head of a society).  Certainly, it should not be any kind of woman, but rather, an individual who would be sensitive enough to human sufferings.  Further, it should also be a female who honors her motherhood qualities, and who can express genuine love to all her constituents.

Furthermore, it should be a swaying female who believes in equality and who is brilliant in diplomacy.  Currently, the Congolese women are in desperate need of a real Mfumu-Nkento (woman head of their society) who would exemplify the strength, as well as the

*Congolese Woman chief (Mfumu Nkento)*

propensity of our ancient queens, who were more focused in preserving their territory as well as their people.  Moreover, women are seeking a Mfumu-Nkento (Woman Chief) who is an eloquent debater, who can negotiate in behalf of her people rather than focusing on self-interests.

In addition to the foregoing qualities, a desired Mfumu-Nkento should also be the one who would remember to restore the educational system of all the children, and that of the adults in every level.  Because children are the foundation of a nation, they need special attention in every step of their lives until they reach the maturity age.  Adult should also be encouraged to acquire more education.  Further, diverse trainings should be made available for the people to choose from, so that they could acquire new knowledge which eventually would help them to cope with modern standard of living.  In general Woman head would look after all the senior citizens; and provide for their needs, because most of them serve us as live librarians in transmitting oral traditions to their successors, immaculately.

A Mfumu-Nkento (Woman Chief) is actually a conservative woman who believes that the new generation should rely more on their oral traditions, because they are authentic, as opposed to other textbooks

*Congolese Woman chief (Mfumu Nkento)*

written by non native. Usually, they conveyed fragmentary information that might have been colored by lack of precise knowledge of the facts involved, as well as a communication gap between two opposite groups of people. A competent woman chief would be the one who believes in restoring legal system of the Congolese modern society in order to put an end to the following problems such as corruption, impunity, scarcity, treachery and deceit; because all these awful things represent the ills or evils in the Congolese modern society. Those things have never been there during their ancestors' time. It would be preferable that they return back to their origin, according to the citizens of this country.

Generally, improving the living condition of a nation such as RDC would require the willingness or the collaboration of a woman head of the nation along with sincere male individuals to come on board develop some strategies of restoring the dreadful condition and implement it thereafter, such as stopping selfishness, and applied generosity, justice, love and respect to every citizen.

*Congolese Woman chief (Mfumu Nkento)*

## CHAPTER 9:

# The Role of a Public Servant

How Does Mfumu-Nkento (Woman Chief) See the Role of a Public Servant?

Being a public servant does not necessary signify that that elected individual is being given the privilege to serve himself or herself.  The role of a public servant is not for self-interests. The role of a public servant is not to merely focus on the welfare of family members, close and distant relatives, as well as their close associates alone.  In fact, ignoring the rest of the people for a decade would cause a serious dilemma in the long run.  Apparently, such practice would be nothing, but the exploitation of the population.  Further, such practice indicates treachery and deceit to the people who have entrusted that individual in governing the citizens, kindly.  Can any population rejoice living under such a brutal environment?  This should absolutely not be the case, if the leader is wise enough, and wants to prevent upheaval.

A public servant ought to develop a high degree of humiliation, and establish mutual communication with its constituents in order to

*Congolese Woman chief (Mfumu Nkento)*

ensure peace, love, respect, justice and integrity.  Naturally, the public is demanding, and that is a normal reaction, because the public is actually the public servant's boss, as it were.  Thus, the public servant should always be held accountable for his or her actions towards its employer, in this respect, the public servant, would be motivated to improve his or her performance, ultimately.

In a Democratic country people need to have a freedom of speech. If citizens are forbidden to voice their opinions, could such system honestly be termed Democratic? Freedom is regarded as a gift from God to His children.  And therefore, any intelligent leader should not deny his people to exercise their rights.

According to the wisdom of Mfumu-Nkento (woman chief) of the former time, she sounded a following warning to her successors: "Beware, people! Know that in the society where people are forbidden to express themselves, they develop intense anger or hostility.  Where there is irritation, the chief cannot establish peace; consequently, the chief begins, gradually, losing his or her credibility and respect.  That usually occurs in sequence, the first layer of respect goes, and then, the next will follow, and so on.  As a result, he becomes powerless or worthless.

*Congolese Woman chief (Mfumu Nkento)*

The respect and authority dissolve from the eyes of those who once had held the chief in a highest *regard.* So it would be wise for any clever individual to become aware that treachery and deceit would cause distrust to the people. So to prevent such thing, egocentricity should be replaced with the practice of philanthropy.

Further, being disrespectful to your fellowman degrades the chief's image. It would be highly recommended for a leader to develop a humanitarian attitude and also strive to improve everyone's standard of living. A leader who would act in this manner would be eventually honored, and the population would speak about this individual with reverence. *This is the reason why we are reminded to treat other people as we would like them to treat us*, so that we could deserve a perpetual respect in every circumstance.

*Congolese Woman chief (Mfumu Nkento)*

## MINIMUM QUALITIES REQUIRED

### Mfumu-Nkento Should Meet Certain Requirements

The reasons why Mfumu-Nkento (woman chief) would require to meet the criteria of becoming a leader in the Contemporary Congolese society is due to the fact that she should first be viewed as being a strong, as well as a powerful individual prior to being entrusted in governing the mass of the people.  Such woman head should also be aware that preserving the land and ensuring the protection of the people are imperative.  Further, this particular individual should also be made aware that an efficient leader does not govern for a deprave purpose of her people, but rather her governance must be to ensure ancestors' virtues in our modern society.  Thus, exhibiting those qualities is mandatory, because directing diverse people of different family background requires brazenness.  The population is composed of people of different temperaments; some are very cooperative, whereas others are hardheaded to obey.  Therefore, the Woman leader is to adhere to the rules set by our ancestors, and re-enforce them as well.

Apparently, this is the reason why in the former Congolese society the following words such as *impunity, corruption, and penury* were unknown to those people.

*Congolese Woman chief (Mfumu Nkento)*

Those terms have just appeared lately in the Bantu society or during our so called modern time.  Certainly, the destitution is a new word in the Congolese society as well; people do not quite understand it either.  For this reason, Mfumu-Nkento (Woman chief) would have to exercise all the abilities required to ensure a positive leadership, indicating the mass of the people, and maintain it continuously.

All the good qualities established by the Congolese ancestors would have to be recalled and practiced, or they should actually be incorporated in our modern life and sustain it.  Modern leaders had unfortunately failed to follow after the Congolese ancestors' footsteps; perhaps, that is due to the fact that most of them are impostors, and had no knowledge of the Congolese culture, so to speak.  *Consequently, the Congolese society is now found in such a chaotic situation which God alone can extricate it.*  Certainly, where there is no law and decency, there is nothing else, but anarchy, and destruction.  Such is the situation which is running rampant in this country, currently.

Our former Mfumu-Nkento disapproved of any kind of repressive leadership, because people develop displeasure, and eventually they can no longer hold their leader in the highest regard.

*Congolese Woman chief (Mfumu Nkento)*

Therefore, it would make it impossible to ensure protection of the people, or attempt to maintain and sustain harmony under such oppressive leadership.  Besides from recognizing those qualities, Mfumu-Nkento insists on the fact that any wise chief should really focus on the good ancestral qualities in order to be able to restore the image of the country as well as to guarantee the real freedom to the population.

# CHAPTER 10

### BANTU ANCESTORS'WEAKNESS

Based on the oral traditions, the Congolese live Historians state that since the colonization of the Kingdom of Kongo which has subsequently evolved to the Democratic Republic of the Congo, they came to realize that the biggest enemy of this land came from the practice of the following elements: 1.- GENEROSITY, 2.- *a high degree of* HOSPITALITY, and 3.- *Blind Faith,* which could actually be translated to Naiveness of the Congolese leaders toward their neighbors and their exploiters or their guests, so called.

*Congolese Woman chief (Mfumu Nkento)*

In essence, these people had always been extremely simple and trustworthy. They surely were lacking critical judgment and analysis in dealing with the outsiders.  In fact, they regarded their guests highly, and especially those who presented themselves as the servants of God (*the early missionaries*), as it were.

Because the Congolese ancestors had always held the name of God (Nzambi-Mpungu) in the highest regard, they had been under the impression that those individuals, who presented themselves in the name of God, were upright.  Little, however, they knew about their deceit or their cunning motive.  The Bantu ancestors were indeed naïve and certainly were lacking a high degree of discernment; so due to their generosity, hospitality, and blind faith, they left their doors wide open to their so called honorable guests; and consequently, they lost their power from 15th century and up to this day!

In fact, since the colonization period, up to these days, the impostors had begun entering the country from left to right, some illegally and others under the guise of refugees, friendship, fake investors, and so on.  As a result, all these individuals had seized this opportunity to usurp the authority of their land.

*Congolese Woman chief (Mfumu Nkento)*

The impostors, viciously, had turned against the citizens of the country who had welcomed them wholeheartedly.  They eventually rejoice in massacring everyone without any apparent cause, including, children and adults, and especially, causing violence against women without any compunction whatsoever in the 21$^{st}$ century where every nation has produced all types of Scholars in the various fields.  The application of the word humanitarian instead of appearing superficial could be strengthened in this day and age by the longing of eradicating the desire for the conquest of one nation against another.

However, nowadays, modern Congolese woman chief would do well if she could acknowledge her predecessors' errors and thereby trying to develop a critical analysis method of dealing with people by modifying the degree of her generosity, hospitality and trust, toward her potential guests as well as all others.

*Congolese Woman chief (Mfumu Nkento)*

# Conclusion

In writing about African culture, notably the Bantu/Congolese culture, our purpose is to highlight the nature of a **Bantu/Congolese woman** overall. We are particularly, describing the qualities of a former Congolese woman chief in terms of the role she had played as a married woman, as a mother, as well as a woman head of a society.

The oral traditions had emphasized the reason why she was empowered in leading her fellowman accurately, and the manner in which she had exercised that power in handling her private and legal affairs appropriately.  Thus, we have exposed her courage, strength and wisdom in embracing every aspect of sociopolitical issues effectively; underlining high qualities and negating those pertaining to immorality. *Below, we will systematically expose all the insightful advices which were revealed to us by our live historians throughout our research.*

When we actually speak about Mfumu-Nkento (woman chief), we are not alleging, by all means that every Congolese woman is empowered in leading the nation.

*Congolese Woman chief (Mfumu Nkento)*

In fact, in ancient time, the title of Mfumu-Nkento to which we had reference was about the courageous woman who usually came from a royal background, and was either forced to take on the task of leading the society or the family from a frail male leader, or it could also be that the title had been inherited for the lack of a senior male individual in that family.  Based on the Bantu's traditions, the transmissions of authority must always be done harmoniously.  There was no implication of any usurpation of the power, because a usurper knew it well that attempting to seize other people's authority was completely forbidden in the Bantu society.  That was definitely viewed as a crime, because it violates ancestors' law; consequently, the usurper would have to face an unexpected death.

In fact, currently, people continue applying the same principle in the villages.  The village chief has to always come from the former royal family of that village.  They follow the social norm and routine in terms of succession; whether a male or a female individual was empowered to lead the society.  However, such individual has to be enthroned prior to taking that responsibility.  The enthronement in fact requires a special ceremony before the sight of everyone.

*Congolese Woman chief (Mfumu Nkento)*

And so it is in all the families; usually, a male senior individual would assume the family leadership. However, should his leadership appears unsatisfactory, a strong, and courageous woman can always be empowered to lead, after being enthroned. Obviously, all those traditional heads should first exemplify the knowledge of the ancestral good qualities prior to taking that step. They have to be viewed as individuals having a considerable power and wisdom to guide others. They should set such a good example in their respective families first, and then, in their villages, as well as in their societies.

In effect, according to oral traditions, the former Mfumu-Nkento, regardless to her title, was a multitasking female; and knew how to prioritize her tasks. As a wife, this **Congolese** Woman Chief (Mfumu-Nkento) **knew exactly** how to honor her marriage's obligations. She remained submissive and respected her husband as the culture requires it. Also, as a mother, she let her conscience guide her about her motherhood's duties. She nurtured her children with a lot of love, and she also taught them how to practice solidarity among themselves. The mother was aware of all the details regarding living in the society which is composed of various individuals. And therefore, she had to ensure

*Congolese Woman chief (Mfumu Nkento)*

in warning her children to remain vigilant against individuals who are engaged in songuer's activities; because songuers' motives are always known to be destructive.

Furthermore, she stressed on the fact that her children should learn how to become self-sufficient, but not lethargic.  She also found it necessary to explain to them the most crucial secret, that "**Nzambe (uhn-Zambah)** - (the great Being or God) had seen your virtues, because of that *H*e had filled the land with a great deal of natural resources.  Although, you might not acquire everything at the same time, remember however that whatever you need could be found in the land, and learn to get it yourselves, and try not to be undervalued by looking outward. You have been privileged, indeed, so, try to always be thankful to your Nzambe/Nzambi-Mpungu/Mungu (our Great Being in Heaven) and also be grateful to our ancestors who had left us this beautiful land, and had kept all the usurpers out, and so, shall you do."

In essence, as far as the ancient society is concerned, their business relationship was well organized.  The system of payments was well established and available to everyone.  In fact, people were allowed to conduct exchanges of their goods or transactions among them.

*Congolese Woman chief (Mfumu Nkento)*

However it was always done harmoniously.  The law prohibited to carry out any contemptible activities of violence and exploitation of other part of life.  Therefore try not to be irrational individuals.

As a mother, the female chief's duty was to whisper in the ears of her children the following secret, "Remember there is something called a **"Curse,"** *it means that anything you have acquired brutally has WINGS, because it was not earned, it shall fly away from you sooner or later, one way or the other in order to return to its pristine origin.  Nevertheless, it will leave you with remorse, afterwards and plus other kinds of entanglements.*

Therefore, it is imperative that you become aware of this ancestral wisdom, so that you could be protected against any future consequences."

However, as a woman chief, she expressed a lot of love, but was firmed in terms of governing the society, and ensuring proper administration, local as well as international.  The Woman Chief was actually aware that people regarded her highly, and therefore, she made certain to guarantee harmony, peace, freedom and protection to her people; so, depravity was unknown.

*Congolese Woman chief (Mfumu Nkento)*

The Congolese live Historians (*referring to our wise senior citizens usually those who came from the royal backgrounds*) suggest the proper manners in which a contemporary Mfumu-Nkento (woman chief) should actually act in terms of leading a modern African nation in order to restore cultural values and maintain them perpetually.  This means that, a female modern chief would need to acquire ancestral good qualities.  She would need also to develop a certain degree of fear from doing evil to others, in order to prevent any sort of *repercussion to her constituents*.  She would have to remember that an authoritarian leadership would be chaotic.

Further, the *live historians/chiefs* had also indicated the types of criteria which a female individual is supposed to honor, nowadays, prior to being entrusted with a title of Mfumu-Nkento (Woman Chief) in the contemporary society.

In fact, we have stressed the Congolese *ancestors' good qualities which kept families, villagers, and the society together; and also, the manner in which the people sustained peace in their families, as well as in the society, in general.*  According to their God's given wisdom, they were aware of why a land produces supply and why would the supply vanished from the land.

*Congolese Woman chief (Mfumu Nkento)*

The Bantu ancestors had revealed and underlined *the practice of integrity, loyalty, justice, love, respect and generosity, because they attract prosperity in the country, whereas, selfishness, greed, cruelty or brutality, and injustice or any malice will* **repel** *wealth from that society, because these ungodly attributes are associated with negative feelings, thereby creating incoherence* within the people.

Furthermore, we have been advised to know that greed will generate cruelty or brutality which in turn will attract *recurrent "***Curse***"* in an individual's life, including family's problems, as well as business failure. The Congolese ancestors for that reason had sounded a warning to their successors, who ignorantly may scoff at their wisdom, which was conveyed through their virtues.

In actual fact, it is because of those qualities that our **Nzambe**/Nzambi-Mpungu/**Mungu** (God the Almighty) continues to pour divine blessings in the land. In truth, those who are defiant would definitely reap their own miseries. And eventually, those miseries would be experienced in their lives, because they would unfortunately join the rest of the people who would be caught in the *cycle of recurring curse.*

*Congolese Woman chief (Mfumu Nkento)*

The word "Curse" perpetuates the singing of the word *"bankruptcy"* in whatever business adventures they might be doing.  As the old saying, '*Prevention is better than cure*."  Remember, however, that a temporary pleasure, which ignorant individuals find by harming others, is just ephemeral, but the curse associated with that vicious activity would remain perpetual.  So you might as well heed this advice and remain free."

*Our oral traditions had actually made this wisdom available to the younger generation.  It is up to them to be able to pick and choose which action they would rather prefer to undertake, and also, know beforehand what consequence to expect from taking such action in the long run.*

Furthermore, we have talked about the Congolese woman's strengths and weaknesses. Her main strength is focused in bringing forth a positive change around her which would be beneficial to everyone involved in her household, as well as in her society.  She strives in fostering a positive change in every aspect such as social, economic development, politic, and religious *without any gender distinction*.  She also believes that everyone *should be treated and respected equally*, so that the world around her may remain happy and harmonious.

*Congolese Woman chief (Mfumu Nkento)*

Additionally, the Congolese woman deems that *selfishness* as the culture stated does indeed generate *anger, or antagonism in the family, as well as in the society.*  However, **"Love**" *alone is an efficient great Weapon that could fight and defeat a giant (enemy) of any kind.  It is also known as the greatest remedy that could cure all sorts of physical and social diseases.  In fact, our traditional law evokes love.*

The younger generation is therefore, recommended to seek every possible means, which would permit the individual to exercise love rather than getting caught in the wrong associations where a group of individuals, giggle cheerfully, while they are knowingly performing *immoral activities*, and ignoring their repercussions in the long run.

In regard to *saving her marriage*, a Congolese woman is too *patient*, and does not act abruptly.  She prefers to wait until the required physical evidence has been made available prior to proceeding with any reported rumors; and especially, when the ''Songuers" or epanza-makita (double agents) are implicated in that situation.  In general, a Congolese woman is a very *spiritual being*; and her faith helps her to bring her stubborn partner to God which would help him to grow spiritually, and also change him to acquire a decent behaviors.

*Congolese Woman chief (Mfumu Nkento)*

Further, the woman's faith helps her to meet any daily challenges. This is how a Congolese woman uses her wisdom in saving her marriage, or in changing negative situations to a positive outcome. She usually goes from a *possible defeat to a mighty victory*. Further, she is known to be humble as well as submissive individual to her spouse. Nonetheless, if she is *exposed to any physical or sexual abuses*, the Congolese woman's decision is in that case, very *unyielding.*

Based on African traditions, if the King proves to be a frail individual, the woman head is empowered to lead the kingdom, because she does not tolerate hedging or viewing perpetual miseries around her. Besides from the above, she had also been instructed that leadership cannot be insubstantial, but it should be led with ingenuity in order to bolster the kingdom's virtues.

In effect, the Congolese ancient society had never disdained the authority of Mfumu-Nkento (Woman Chief), because gender was not regarded as a barrier for a woman to ensure the leadership in the society. The recognition of good qualities was a prerequisite, in addition to her outspokenness or bluntness to stop any dreadful situations which might be infiltrating at that particular moment.

*Congolese Woman chief (Mfumu Nkento)*

However, African women, especially the Congolese women continue to face political struggle from colonial era to these days. And yet, during the pre-colonial epoch, the Congolese woman' voice was heard in the entire society and in the family settings. This is where the title of Mfumu-Nkento (woman head) was originated. We believe that restoring African women historical image is necessary. **The question asked**: *But who's going to do it*? **Answer**: *Obviously, it is up to the women themselves.* True, nowadays, many women are willing to embrace the position of trust, provided that they are given the opportunities to do so. The barriers apparently come from self-centered male individuals, probably due to their immaturity and incompetence in handling domestic and international relationship, and therefore they feel threatened by those who have acquired the ability to fill those positions of trust.

As we have discussed earlier in this book, during the ancient time the criteria had to be met, prior to being entrusted with the title of honor, or to sit on that throne. The woman's assertiveness to command and to defend were also the added qualities which had to permit a female in complying with Mfumu-Nkento (Woman Chief)'s obligations.

*Congolese Woman chief (Mfumu Nkento)*

Nowadays, in the Congolese society, these principles are practiced, specifically, in the villages, as well as in their family settings.  It would be suggested that in this day and age gender issue be eliminated, so that any individual who meets the qualifications required to assume the position of trust be allowed without any reservation.

Because the Congolese culture had never reported any gender issue, in terms of assuming any social leadership, it would be fair to the Congolese modern society to stop adopting any gender discrimination in the current political system.  The leadership of our modern nation should be open to both male and female individuals who exhibit a high degree of competency or whoever who meets the qualifications required, as long as that individual remains focused on the ancestral recommendations, such as ensuring solidarity, instead of alienating other people involved in the society.  Additionally, that prospective leader would have to prove also that he or she is strong enough to re-inforce any law such as the law against carrying out act of violence in the society or even exploiting other part of life.

Furthermore, that potential individual would have to implement all the social regulations required. That would include making it mandatory

*Congolese Woman chief (Mfumu Nkento)*

for every individual to become self-sufficient, but not beggars, because of the fact that the land is prosperous, and therefore no one would be permitted to undervalue himself or herself.

It would be therefore a fallacy for anyone to maintain a lethargic attitude in such a society. However, that does not imply that individuals may not be in need of anything sometimes. Should that be the case, individuals are allowed to conduct any exchange of any items needed at that particular time, with other fellow beings in the society, provided that the exchange is conducted in such harmonious and respectable manner. Overall, the Congolese culture encourages people to be self-sufficient in order to reflect a respectable image.

*The fundamental ancestral virtues which had been orally transmitted to the new generation, such as: integrity, loyalty, justice, generosity, fidelity, protection, respect, and love ought to be stressed at all times in the minds of our younger people. Oral traditions also had highlighted the word "**Selfishness**."* We have been advised that selfishness should not be practiced in the society, because it causes social illness.

*Congolese Woman chief (Mfumu Nkento)*

A peacefully society consists of generous people. This is the reason why the Congolese culture stresses more on generosity, loyalty, caring, sharing, love, respect, justice, and hospitality, in order to maintain a happy society where you can bring forth happy individuals, ready to comply with the norms and regulations, and not to be defiant.

The wisdom of the Congolese ancestors requires that in order to ensure peace around the family as well as in the society, a wise leader or a public servant, is required to develop a humble or modest disposition, because arrogance generates disrespect approach, and it also creates resistance, disobedience, and anarchy which makes it very difficult to guide or command appropriately.  Therefore, a clever leader would not deprive its people from their God's given freedom.

Mfumu- Nkento (woman chief) had advised the strategy of leading your family and the society ingeniously.  In fact, she focused on the following, "*It would be wise allowing a population to express itself* that would entail the adoption of a democratic rather than an autocratic system.  Furthermore, listening to your people attentively is quite necessary.

*Congolese Woman chief (Mfumu Nkento)*

Ultimately, it would be wise addressing any concern courteously. *Some questions or statements are thoughts provoking, and should be handled delicately.* Additionally, any brilliant leader should actually learn how to make intelligent decisions, based on the needs of the population and make the implementation, shortly thereafter.

Moreover, the traditional law underlined another topic which the younger generation, in the Congolese society, should remember carefully as long as they live in this world, "***Never to mock the wisdom of their ancestors, because it was inspired by Nzambi-Mpungu (God the Almighty), and was never originated by the little gods.*** They sounded a warning in the term '*Curse*", and how it is transmitted from the author of that evil to the rest of the family members in the future generation.

There are diverse activities in life which can generate a *curse* in somebody's life, according to the Congolese predecessors; therefore, this word has become almost redundant in the ears of the younger people, because it needs to be imbedded in their minds, so that they would refrain from acting naughtily.

*Congolese Woman chief (Mfumu Nkento)*

The well known advice is, "***Never to seize anything that belongs to somebody else, cruelly, because that generates a negative force in your life***, **and will eventually** *create a link of recurrent Curse from your end to the other end.*

Actually that shall be a recurrence activity which shall stop your blessings and bring you unpleasant situations to handle, so long as you shall live in this world.  And therefore, ***be no part of the disgraceful conditions***.  Do not attempt to imitate other societies' cultures that may rationalize contemptible activities, or believing in impunity.  Such thinking would not stop the *wheel of curse and its perpetual reactions*. You shall remember to repeatedly recite the good qualities which your ancestors had transmitted to you: *Integrity, loyalty, generosity, justice, fidelity, compassion, love, and respect.*  Besides from those virtues, you shall ensure hospitality to your neighbors, and never to harm anyone, **except in self-defense**; that is when you shall actually be ***ADAMANT*!

In effect, this should be the appropriate time to begin reading between the lines and make your selection of genuine friends from those fiendish individuals.  These qualities shall always help you and bring you close to Nature.

*Congolese Woman chief (Mfumu Nkento)*

Seeing your pure heart, with no slightest desire to harm any other part of life, Nzambi-Mpungu (God the Almighty) will then, shower your country with every type of wealth.

In addition, you should remember to remain unyielding and be anchored in your oral traditions, because they were meant to be immaculately transmitted to our successors.

Additionally, you shall ensure not to duplicate other people's errors, because that would certainly contaminate our good qualities, because it is obligatory that those qualities be kept at their pristine state and be passed on to the next generation unmistakably.  In essence, it would be mandatory to all the Congolese live historians (*senior citizens from the royal background*) and the contemporary Congolese scholars, to be able to chronologically record all the current social events, systematically and accurately, so that they may be transmitted unspoiled to your new generation, as this would prevent any types of confusions in the future.  Furthermore, any individual who shall be anchored in his or her traditions would eventually not be engaged in deceptive negotiations with his or her fellowman, because that would definitely not be the means of promoting those high cultural qualities, such as integrity.

*Congolese Woman chief (Mfumu Nkento)*

Again, you should remain anchored in your own oral traditions, and do not let anyone sway you in believing in any other unauthentic material. Should such thing be presented to you, you may read it, but sparingly; however *be unyielding to any discrepancy or to any fragmentary information reported by anyone who had a slightest knowledge of your own culture, because such an individual is inclined to amplify negativity and conceal the reality.* **Evidently, diverse people** were given different cultures from yours. This is why people should always be referred to their own origin in order to obtain authentic information regarding their backgrounds.

Ultimately, concerning women, Mfumu-Nkento had put an emphasis on the following recommendations, "Remember to always be patient as a woman and a mother of the society in order to prevent your leadership being as inefficient as the one from a self-centered male leader which most of the time results to injustice.

Above all, be wise and always turn to your **Nzambe**/Nzambi-Mpungu (*God the Almighty*) to seek guidance and wisdom in dealing with your fellowman. In fact, having such disposition would help you in determining how you should exactly read between the lines when facing an opponent or any confusion.

*Congolese Woman chief (Mfumu Nkento)*

Thus, being alert when facing unclear situations is necessary; this is how you could be able to determine the validity of any statement which is being made before you, and which would eventually necessitate your wise decision.

Sometimes, such statement could be viewed as an *omen that could prevent you acting unwisely, rather than acting* diplomatically in some cases, or to be blunted under certain circumstances, if necessary in order to stop right then and there any negative implications.

Evidently, past experience, good or bad would always serve as a lesson in the future.  Apparently individuals become wise in dealing with others, distinguishing the real friends from their foes afterwards.

Further, our live historians reported that our ancestors in fact, had advised their successors of the following: "The preservation of the land is essential, because it is Nzambe (God)'s gift to Its people.  We, the predecessors had done our part.  You shall do yours.  You shall love and protect your land, as well as your resources – Also, remember that:

 *"The leadership of this country is not the food that you would offer your guests today, and then forget about it thereafter!*

*Congolese Woman chief (Mfumu Nkento)*

*So beware!  Mopaya" is an impostor –a usurper, he penetrates cunningly and collaborates with a treason who is a disloyal and unworthy individual, who has no position in the land, except self-interested motive!"*

Finally, as a leader, you should follow the suitable means of promoting assistance to your constituents in order to improve their standards of living.  By doing so, you would create a peaceful society.

The secret of being a successful leader is to always be wise and humble, especially be a good listener.  It is necessary to realize that adopting an autocratic disposition would be nothing, but robbing people's freedom.

In fact, any leader who would act in such a shameful manner would automatically lose all the layers of respect from which he or she had been initially enfolded, because as we have said it, "**BOTOSI** (*boh-toh-se*) or **LUZITU** (lou-ze –tou)"or Respect must be earned, so strive to earn it.  And then, make sure to maintain and sustain it.

Ultimately, with respect to contemporary African women, the voice of a modern Congolese woman should be heard nowadays, because the same ability and intelligence she had during the ancient time, she still has it.

*Congolese Woman chief (Mfumu Nkento)*

A bright woman was given the insight to perceive ahead of time what is going to be needed, and how she can use her own perception to restore the situations without any delay.

Currently, a female scholar is well equipped to revamp all the institutions in the nation such as schools, hospitals or fostering economic development, and addressing any social or political issues.  Her aim is to actually provide a high standard of living to the entire society.

Presently, a modern Congolese woman is just requesting an opportunity to exercise her wisdom, intelligence, skills as well as all her maternal abilities in order to ensure appropriate governance.

Additionally, as an African woman, who is anchored in her traditions, regardless to her position of trust which she might acquire in her society, respect and the submissive attitude towards her spouse could never be ignored.

In fact, doing so would be a fallacy to traditional law.  Ultimately, due to her maternal disposition, as well as to her multitasking abilities, a contemporary Congolese woman head of a nation, who has met all the necessary requirements involved, we estimate would be capable to

*Congolese Woman chief (Mfumu Nkento)*

embrace both socio-economic matters as well as sociopolitical aspects effectively.  She would also be able to bring about a positive change, thereby, ensuring peace, justice, harmony, love, and safety in a working environment where male and female individuals could work joyously together in order to become more productive; and eventually, become self-sufficient and restore the family values as the Bantu/Congolese society requires it.

**FINIS**

## BEPONA BOOKS

# *Africa Presents*

- *The Congo RDC and Lingala Language (English and French version ( First edition)* - **LINGALA DICTIONARY - by Bepona Collection**

- *The Congo RDC and Kikongo ya l'Etat Language (English and French version (first edition).* - **KIKONGO ya l'Etat DICTIONARY - by Collection**

- *The Congo RDC and Child Education (First edition)*

- *The Congo RDC and Congolese Cuisine (First edition)*

- *The Congo RDC and A Congolese Woman Chief (Mfumu-Mkento)*

- *The Congo RDC Et la Femme Dirigeante (Mfumu-Nkento)*

- *The Congo RDC and Congolese Tradition Law (first edition)*

- *The Congo RDC and Congolese Comedy/Novel*

    1.  *A Mysterious Boy called Timo Mikwaya Well known as Kamina*

    2.  *Mr. Aleyi-Atondi*

        *How can this man live with his In-laws for over 15 years?*

    3.  *A Western Professor with an African University Student (Abelengezi)*

    4.  *Experience of two African young ladies in America (Magoke)*

    *By*

    *Bepona Collection*

# Books' Samples

Africa presents the Congo RDC and A **Traditional law/common law.**

Africa presents the Congo RDC and **Child Education in the Bantu society**

Africa presents the Congo RDC and **Congolese Cuisine**

Africa presents the Congo RDC and Lingala Language English French versions

Africa presents the Congo RDC and Kikongo ya l'Etat English and French versions

## ABOUT BEPONA COLLECTION

*The authors of BeponaBooks are female Congolese-American.  We write about the culture of the Bantu society of the Congo RDC, which is located in Central Africa - (MPA, PAS, BBA, and BA).*

*In essence, our books are apolitical. They are based on our personal research conducted scholarly and confirmed by oral traditions of the Bantu peoples, transmitted to us by our live Historians.  In fact, the live historians are the wise living senior citizens who continue to maintain and sustain the authenticity of the oral traditions without any distortion.*  Generally, we concentrate our books on presenting the Congolese culture, which encompasses general social issues.  Evidently, our contemporary history is connected to our ancient traditions.  And therefore, we cannot omit touching some other topics, although slightly-sometimes-when we write about Congolese culture

*Our readers will notice that the titles of all our books in English are prefaced with, "Africa Presents the Congo RDC," and then, are followed by the actual book titles.  The titles of all our books in French are prefaced with, "L'Afrique Présente Le Congo RDC," and then, followed by the actual book titles.  Actually, we purposely took this approach, because we realize that not everyone is proficient in Geography.  Apparently, certain individuals still believe that Africa is a country rather than a Continent.  It is therefore, necessary to clarify the fact that the Congo RDC is a country within this particular Continent and not the other way around.*

*In writing about the Bantu/Congolese culture, we opted to focus on the most important social topics, namely, "Traditional law (Common law), Congolese woman's leadership, Congolese cuisine, and Child education. We also have developed two major Congolese languages (Called Lingala and Kikongo ya l'Etat, that including their respective dictionaries. These languages are spoken in three or four other African countries.*

*All our books are written in simple terms, language and style.  Our goal is to share our culture with individuals, who are interested in diversity, and to express ourselves, but not to impress our readers. Ultimately, in regard to the bibliography, we owe all our credits to the Bantu live historians from the Democratic Republic of the Congo RDC.*

## ACKNOWLEDGMENT

We are grateful to our ancient Congolese women who had exemplified their love, courage, strength, intelligence, and wisdom in dealing with human beings as well as the entire social and the political issues, in such a wisely and victoriously manner. We give recognition to our ancestors, especially to our traditional law (common law), which began acknowledging a woman as an intelligent being, and also as a mother of a society who should be held in the highest regard. This in fact, was due to her ingenuity of managing her household along with many other social responsibilities efficiently. In effect, it has been perceived that when the colonization of the African nations has sought all the necessary means of concealing the truth of this matter, the oral traditions had in that respect disclosed every detail of it; thereby encouraging Contemporary Congolese women to awaken, and begin to get involved in restoring their hidden moral values, as well as revamping all the social institutions that have been destroyed for a decade, and which had been replaced by unethical behaviors.

Above all, we are eternally grateful to our **Nzambe**/Nzambi-Mpungu/***Mungu*** (*The Great Being in heaven*) for endowing his wisdom to the ancient Congolese women. Further, we are thankful to God for having inspired the Congolese men of that era in acknowledging the clever woman's qualities, as well as heeding her motherhood advice. Our ancestors strongly believed that the brilliant woman's role was not limited to just handling household activities, she was rather a multitasking individual capable to fully control all the situations, which were arising around her. Due to this acknowledgment, in the Bantu culture, a woman ought to be addressed with a title of respect, such as "*Mother*," because she represents the mother of our society; and all the highest qualities are embedded in her heart. And therefore, the governance of a Mfumu-Nkento or female Ruler is considered to be very effective.

# KINSHASA, *THE CAPITAL CITY OF THE CONGO RDC*

*PRIOR TO THE CIVIL
WAR*

# M. A. P

# AFRICA

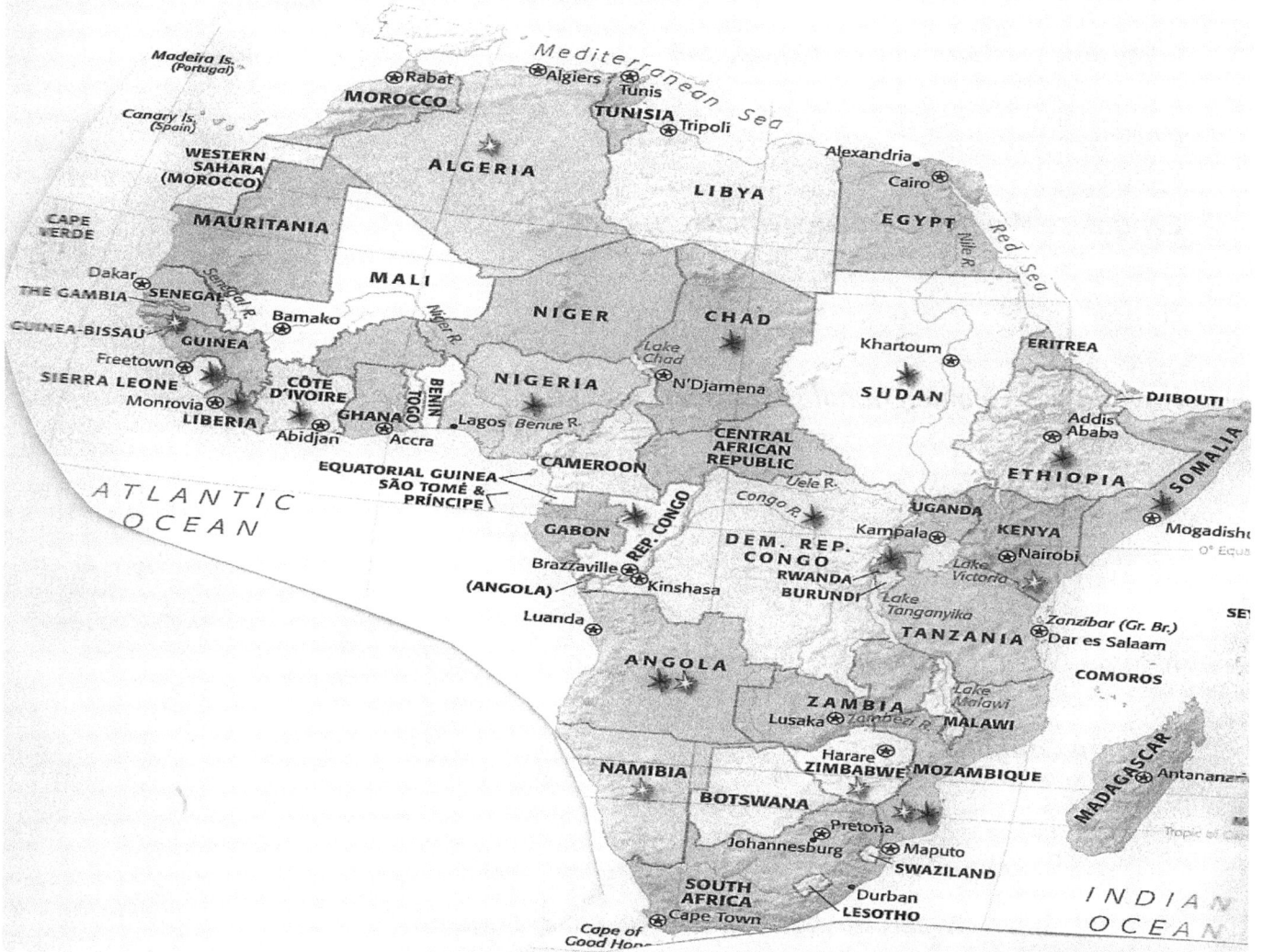

*INDEX*

*B*

*Bantu ancestors' weaknes, ch. 10, page 146*

*C*

*Congolese Woman's productivity, ch. 3, page 34*

*H*

*How do wise women handle "Songuers' activities"?*

*ch. 4, page 40*

*M*

*Mfumu-Nkento (Congolese woman Chief), ch. 1, page 20*

*Modern Congolese Mfumu, ch. 7, page 97*

*R*

*Relationship between Husband and Wife, ch. 2, page 28*

*Q*

*Qualities and Attributes, ch. 6, page 85*

*S*

*T*